First Gener.   Entry
into Higher Education

SRHE and Open University Press Imprint

Current titles include:

First Generation Entry into Higher Education

An International Study

Liz Thomas and Jocey Quinn

Society for Research into Higher Education
& Open University Press

Open University Press
McGraw-Hill Education
McGraw-Hill House
Shoppenhangers Road
Maidenhead
Berkshire
England
SL6 2QL

email: enquiries@openup.co.uk
world wide web: www.openup.co.uk

and Two Penn Plaza, New York, NY 10121–2289, USA

First published 2007

A catalogue record of this book is available from the British Library

ISBN-13: 978 0335 21790 8 (pb) 978 0335 21791 5 (hb)
ISBN-10: 0335 21790 7 (pb)   0335 21791 5 (hb)

Library of Congress Cataloging-in-Publication Data
CIP data has been applied for

Typeset by RefineCatch Limited, Bungay, Suffolk
Printed in the UK by Bell & Bain Ltd, Glasgow

The McGraw-Hill Companies

Contents

List of tables

1

Introduction to the book

Improving equity in higher education

Participation in tertiary education has expanded throughout the world, especially in OECD countries. In many national systems mass participation has been reached, but there are still pronounced inequalities in the patterns of access by traditionally under-represented groups (Skilbeck and Connell 2000). Participation in higher education (HE) especially is associated with privilege and enhanced life opportunities, including improved social standing, employment and earnings, civic participation, cultural engagement, health and life expectancy. Many countries therefore express their concern to improve the equality of opportunities afforded by higher education, to enable people from a wider range of backgrounds to benefit.

> The dominant reason cited for promoting greater HE equity relates to the needs of the economy. This can be contrasted with non-instrumental perspectives that promote the personal and social benefits of learning. These two approaches may converge when education, including HE, is anticipated to contribute to overcoming social exclusion
>
> (OECD 1999)

The OECD (1999) identifies three ways in which learning can help counter-act disadvantage: learning to meet basic needs, learning to facilitate labour market participation and learning to promote social engagement and action. However, in the international policy and implementation arena the emphasis has tended to fall on employment, rather than social engagement and transformation. This, we feel, has a tendency to reduce and narrow the role of higher education, which impacts detrimentally on some of the traditional benefits of HE, which thus are being denied to new cohorts of students.

However, we are also experiencing a time of contestation as to the nature and purpose of Higher Education. Is HE for high quality training; for induction into citizenship; for intellectual excellence; for social transformation; or put most critically is it simply a distraction from the dismantling of public life

and services and a tool for the reproduction of privilege? For some, HE will be a vocational education into a prestigious profession, such as law or medicine, much as it has always been. For others, it provides less elite vocational elements that once were delivered in other contexts, such as nursing. The take up of these provisions will be classed, raced and gendered. In less clearly vocational disciplines a utilitarian ethos has also permeated. Liberal humanist ideas about the educated person seem to persist but shaped more by the discourse of citizenship. Notions of intellectual risk-taking, combined with personal experimentation, have not disappeared, but sit uncomfortably with ideas of consumer comfort and the assured delivery of results. The debate also has a geographical dimension. The increasing trend, among first generation students in particular, to go to local universities and remain at home means that the physical move to another place and domestic structure disappears and with it many of the adventures associated with that transition. The conclusion must be that we are less and less clear what entering HE actually means or implies. With this uncertainty comes opportunity, however, and the impetus to consider university education through an international lens. We hope that this book will therefore be a timely intervention into debates about widening participation and social exclusion.

An initial challenge for an international perspective is the alternative ways in which the field of study – higher education – is defined, as the terminology, policy emphasis and target groups vary between countries. This issue is discussed in more detail in Chapter 2. In this book we focus on higher education, as opposed to broader notions of tertiary education (see Chapter 2, pp. 20–21). A second area of difference is in relation to the language used to describe improving the equity of participation in higher education. We have opted for the term 'widening participation', which embraces the notion of broadening diversity in higher education, rather than simply increasing the number who enter HE. The focus therefore is on engaging people from groups who are currently under-represented in higher education. Widening participation also incorporates the idea not just of 'access' to HE, but of facilitating student success too. Success is defined differently within different higher education systems (for example, completing modules; passing assessments; progressing to the next level of study, continuous study for a specific period of time; graduation; etc.) Furthermore, 'success' may also have alternative meanings for different students – who may have varying motivations for engaging in HE study. Effective widening participation requires students from under-represented groups to have the opportunity to succeed in higher education, rather than just to enter it. Underpinning this book is a belief that if access is not accompanied by student success, claims of 'widened participation' or 'social justice' are insincere. Furthermore, the system may need to be radically altered to redefine success, for example by making it far more flexible – as we discuss in Chapter 6.

Research confirms that widening participation is most effective when it is targeted on specific groups who are under-represented in HE. Different

countries however have varying widening participation target groups. These include:

- Lower socio-economic status
- Minorities: students from alternative country of origin, language, ethnic group or religion to the majority
- Disabled students
- Adult, mature or second chance entrants
- Gender (especially in relation to specific discipline areas)
- Rural or isolated students
- Indigenous groups

Moreover, these groups are defined in different ways within alternative national systems. This is discussed in Chapter 2. This book seeks to refocus the widening participation debate to look more closely and analytically at a missing category: first generation entrants.

International research study

Our book draws on international comparative research to explore the access and success of under-represented groups in tertiary education through the lens of 'first generation entrants'. We undertook an international comparative study about access and success of students from a range of targeted groups (Thomas and Quinn 2003a). The aim of the study was to develop understanding about participation and retention in tertiary education of these student groups, in order to assist national systems and education institutions to support them to succeed.

Researchers were drawn from ten countries: Australia, Canada, Croatia, Germany, Ireland, Netherlands, Norway, Sweden, UK and US. We looked at widening participation in relation to a number of under-represented groups: lower socio-economic groups (SEGs); minorities (including students from alternative country of origin, language or racial group from majority); students with disabilities; and mature students. We developed an innovative methodology (discussed in Chapter 2), which sought to: challenge our own assumptions about problems, solutions and education systems and structures; theorize the experiences of students from specific under-represented groups; and examine alternative policy solutions and interventions.

Our analysis suggested that parental education is a key factor contributing to the access and success of students, but that insufficient attention is paid to this by national systems and institutional interventions. Empirical research from the participating countries indicates that parental education is more important in determining access to HE than employment or financial status, and has a profound impact in relation to other types of targeted groups. For example, the participation in HE by ethnic minorities or students with disabilities is often mediated by parental education. Although closely linked to social class and not implying an individualistic deficit model, educational

background has its own significant dimensions. However, within the HE literature, first generation entry tends to be elided with social class, and it lacks interrogation in its own right. This book demonstrates that when first generation entry is used as a lens it disrupts the taken for granted categories of all the target groups used in widening participation and helps produce much more effective approaches to targeting access and supporting student success. The book therefore provides an innovative perspective on a crucially important but neglected HE concern.

UK qualitative study

In this book we are also drawing on a recent UK wide qualitative study on working class students and their 'drop out' from university (Quinn et al. 2005). The research was funded by the Joseph Rowntree Foundation, and was initiated while all members of the core research team were based at the Institute for Access Studies at Staffordshire University, and involving partners at three other UK universities. It explores the paradox that even in universities offering high levels of support, in localities where jobs are difficult to find, working class students are still 'dropping out', or leaving higher education before completing their target award.

The overall goal of the research was to both understand the meanings and implications of 'voluntary drop out' among working class students, aged under 25, and offer new perspectives and potential solutions to the issues raised. The research involved four post-1992 universities from England, Scotland, Wales and Northern Ireland, identifying them as part of their local and national communities, not as isolated entities. All the universities involved in the study are committed to widening participation and student support. They have targeted working class students and recruit heavily from their local areas and sub-regions. Higher Education Funding Council for England (HEFCE) data shows that all four institutions exceed their benchmarks for recruitment from social classes 111M, IV and V for young full time degree students (HEFCE 2003). Each university strives to offer induction, learning, teaching and assessment that is suitable for their non-traditional student populations, and provides additional student services, including academic and pastoral support. Furthermore, they have all conducted research and initiated projects to improve student retention and success. Nevertheless, they all have significant levels of 'drop out' of working class students. In addition, they are all located in areas which have experienced a decline in traditional industries such as pottery, mining, shipbuilding, engineering and textiles. These localities experience significant problems of poverty and unemployment and each is commonly perceived as 'a gloomy area with social difficulties' (jury day) (see Chapter 6, pp. 81–82 for explanation of term, 'jury day'). This means that it is less easy to assume that these students are tempted away by high salaries, or are being poached by local employers.

It is widely acknowledged that: 'there is a scarcity of data about the causes of non completion by target group students' (UUK 2002: 151), and that many of the problems encountered are methodological. Our research therefore attempted to address the short-comings of previous studies and develop a more appropriate approach. We sought to maximize participation and attempted to involve ex-students using a range of qualitative methods including research jury days (which are events involving a range of stakeholders who present their perspective on a set of key questions posed by the researchers – in this case on the meanings and impacts of 'drop out'), interviews with students who had 'dropped out', an international colloquium, and interviews with careers staff and employment agencies (for a more detailed discussion of methodology see Chapter 6). As part of the project, we created a sample of 67 first generation students aged under 25 whom we were able to interview in depth about their HE experiences: of these 40 were young men and 27 young women. In this book we have been able to draw on this data to build a nuanced qualitative picture of first generation entry and to supplement and co-interrogate our international study.

Overview of the contents of this book

As indicated in the preceding discussion, Chapter 2 explores the research context and methodology that informs the study which is the primary focus of this book. The methodology is innovative, and therefore offers a new perspective on undertaking research about the widening of participation, and it is relevant to understanding the rest of the book, as it delineates the breadth of material included; the processes used to collect the material and its analysis; and the limitations the approaches used involve. Furthermore, the chapter discusses the boundaries of the research by questioning and discussing what is meant by higher education, student success and target groups in the participating countries.

First, the chapter considers the need for international comparative higher education research by considering the global development of higher education. Second, it identifies the problems with traditional approaches and existing research in the field of access and widening participation, which is numerically oriented (and therefore ignores the many qualitative differences); does not seek integrated analysis (presumably because of these difficulties); or undertakes limited comparative analysis (e.g. of two or three countries). Third, the chapter turns to the challenges of undertaking international comparative research, and the need to develop a methodology that is meaningful at both a broader level and in relation to national and local situations. We thus review the role of situated knowledge as a means of avoiding the danger of adopting a very simplistic approach of 'cherry picking' ideas from other countries and transplanting them with little or no cognisance of the national and local context. We therefore consider the importance of situated knowledge as this helps to understand the choice of

research methodology in this study and is an important aspect of the theoretical underpinnings of this work. Fourth, we provide details about our research strategy, including the use and importance of indigenous researchers to enhance understanding of others, but also to promote mutual learning. In other words, much is learnt by reflecting and explaining your own situation to others, rather than simply from descriptions from other research participants. A further aspect of our method is 'multi-layering', in other words not just examining national policies but also considering institutional and student perspective and using insider knowledge to enhance this process. The chapter proceeds by outlining the research tools that were developed to facilitate mutual learning and multi-layering, and we review the advantages and disadvantages of these methods and the research strategy as a whole. We conclude this chapter by reflecting on how this methodology provides new insights which permeate and shape the book.

Chapter 3 reviews the access and success of students from lower socio-economic groups in higher education. This demonstrates that although groups are defined differently in countries participating in our study, there are some commonalities and differences. Students from lower socio-economic groups are defined and targeted in all ten of the countries involved in our study (Thomas and Quinn 2003a: 90). Socio-economic status however is defined in different ways: according to employment, income, geography or parental education; all of which emphasize different issues that impact on the students' access to, and experience in, higher education (discussed further in Chapters 5 and 6). What is particularly interesting to note however is that despite these different ways of defining and targeting students from lower socio-economic groups, they remain under-represented in higher education in each of these countries (Thomas and Quinn 2003a: 92, 89). However, lower rates of success (retention and achievement) are not always associated with these groups and higher rates of withdrawal are not inevitable (Thomas and Quinn 2003a: 106). This suggests that there are significant common challenges relating to the recruitment and admission of these students into higher education, but there are potential benefits to exploring the experience of these students once they are in the higher education system. In particular, we believe that greater emphasis on 'first generation entrants' may contribute to improving both the access and success of students who are currently under-represented in higher education, and in some countries have lower rates of success within HE.

Chapter 4 outlines and develops our theoretical understandings of first generation entry drawing on socio-cultural literature on the family. First it addresses the fact that first generation entry is surprisingly little discussed in international literature on widening participation. Although many studies include first generation entrants, first generation itself is not the explicit focus of debate. Similarly we have not found an adequate theoretical definition of what a first generation is and what this means. Our international study suggests that while first generation entry is intertwined with issues of social class, the impacts of parental education warrant a focused

investigation. We then proceed to provide a workable definition of first generation entry which recognizes changes in the family, changes in patterns of participation in higher education and the interrelation with social class. We argue that first generation entrants are those for whom the older responsible generation (not necessarily biological parents) have not had an opportunity for university study at any time in their lives.

The chapter proceeds to develop a conceptual picture of first generation entry. It discusses current debates about the fluidity of family life and the change from emphasis on structures to interest in relationships. Using qualitative data from the UK study introduced above, it questions the applicability of theories of family fragmentation and individualization to first generation entry. Instead it argues that our findings concur much more with theories of reciprocal and moral relationships within families. It agrees with the argument that rather than producing generalizations about families we need to look at the situated processes by which they are produced as subjects. To do this in the case of first generation entry we have focused on the dominant discourses and practices of transition to higher education and explored how they produce students and their families as certain kinds of subjects.

We do not see families as passive in this process but rather as already possessing sources of social capital; albeit social capital that is not always recognized or respected within universities. We discuss how first generation entry can be used to build the family store of bonding, bridging, linking and imagined social capital, but argue that this process is messy and far from straightforward. There is a tension between the desire for family mobility and loyalty to the family and this produces first generation entry as an ambivalent process. We use theories of 'sociological ambivalence' to discuss this ambivalence and also draw on cultural notions of 'memory' to understand its nuances. We conclude this chapter by establishing first generation entry as a complex, dynamic and multi-level process. This understanding then informs our ongoing discussions throughout the book.

Chapter 5 examines the potential impact of parental education on access and success in higher education through an examination of international literature, research, data, policies and interventions. It is argued that the way in which socio-economic status is defined (according to income, employment, geography or parental education) gives differential weight to economic and cultural capital, and thus shapes the types of policies and interventions that are implemented to improve access to higher education and success within HE. This is illustrated through examples of different national strategies to widen participation in higher education. The research evidence is then discussed about the role of economic and cultural barriers to entry and success in higher education. Few would disagree that finance can operate as a major deterrent to participation in higher education, but the extent of the negative impact is unclear, and studies have produced contradictory findings. More significantly however, there is discussion about whether the real barrier is finance or, rather, concerns about spending or borrowing money to fund higher education. The latter is related to the extent to which higher

education is valued, and this may be strongly influenced by parental educational background.

Parental education and cultural attitudes can be understood to have far greater implications than on attitudes towards student debt. Parental education tends to result in material advantage and it forms, either directly or indirectly, many decisions which shape a young person's life. For example, it will inform family spending decisions and priorities, neighbourhood of residence, and nurseries and schools that are selected as well attitudes and values towards education. Parental education can also, to some extent, reduce the negative impact of other factors. Thus, research evidence suggests that parental education has an important impact on early child development and school achievement.

School achievement and attitudes towards learning are directly related to participation in post-secondary education, which in turn influences progression to higher education. In the UK for example, the majority of qualified applicants are progressing to higher education. Transition and experiences within higher education are also highly influenced by parental education and cultural capital that is transmitted to their children. For example, children from families with a history of higher education have access to better information to inform their higher education choices, and they have more informed and realistic expectations about higher education. They are also more likely to fit in with peers, and feel more integrated socially. This chapter therefore suggests that parental education plays an important role in determining and supporting access to, and success in, higher education.

Chapter 6 uses our UK-wide qualitative study of the 'drop out' of first generation students to provide an in depth account of the influence of parental education on the experiences of entering, studying within and ultimately withdrawing from higher education. The chapter introduces the research project explaining how a qualitative participative methodology was employed to produce detailed accounts of drop out from the perspectives of first generation entrants themselves. It explains how the interview process focused explicitly on parental education and attitudes to higher education and their impact on subsequent university experiences.

The chapter demonstrates that these are fluid families that do not fall into traditional structures. It shows that although parents had not had the opportunity of university education themselves, they wanted this for their children and in many respects welcomed the opportunities for family mobility. They did not lack aspirations, but they could not ignore the structural constraints of poverty and class. They wanted their children to have access to education that protected family survival and sustainability, and had to set limits to that participation in terms of where their children could study or live. University education was by no means considered essential to a happy or fulfilled life and it was seen in terms of doing something useful rather than being someone different.

The chapter proceeds to show how parental lack of opportunity for university education and lack of knowledge about university norms and systems

impacts negatively on student ability to enter, progress and even stay in university. However, it also demonstrates the ways in which parents attempted to help and support their children as best they could. It shows that it was parents whom students turned to and trusted for guidance when it came to decisions about both entering HE and leaving early. Although commonly seen as a life crisis this was mostly a rational decision to leave, generally with the hope to return at a more suitable time and for a more appropriate course of study. In this process family harmony was valued over and above the merits of staying unhappily in university. Parents displayed flexibility and contingency and both parents and students desired more flexible options rather than being tied irrevocably to three years uninterrupted study. We argue that perhaps they are the real life long learners and institutions and policy makers need to catch up with them. The chapter concludes that institutional interventions are necessary both to overcome the particular problems faced by first generation entrants and to transform the system to respond to their needs. The following chapter proceeds to consider how this is being addressed internationally.

Chapter 7 explores national and institutional approaches to supporting first generation entrants to access and succeed in higher education. The chapter includes a discussion about alternative ways in which widening participation is conceptualized, and the implications these have on the interventions that are developed and implemented. Drawing on our international research study, the chapter examines some of the different ways in which widening participation is being addressed. These are critiqued in relation to the underlying principles, and the extent to which they address the interests of first generation entrants are assessed. This international analysis reveals that there is very little explicit recognition of the impact of parental education in many national and institutional efforts to widen participation, and when first generation entrants are named, the specific and direct influences of parental background are not fully considered.

The first part of the chapter identifies and conceptualizes alternative approaches to widening participation: the academic approach, the utilitarian approach and the transformative approach (Jones and Thomas 2005). The academic approach focuses on a relatively narrow group of students from under-represented groups who have the academic potential to enter and succeed in higher education, but lack either the aspirations or information to access HE. Thus these potential students are constructed as being in deficit with regard to these qualities, problematic and in need of 'fixing'. Thus widening participation initiatives informed by the academic discourse focus on supporting these students to enter higher education, with little or no concern about their experience within HE; they address individual attitudinal issues rather than structural barriers to participation. The second approach to widening participation that is considered is utilitarian discourse, which focuses on the need for higher education to better meet the needs of the economy. Thus, potential entrants may be viewed as not only lacking aspirations and information to enter higher education, but they may not

have appropriate qualifications or academic preparation either, and may face other structural barriers to access and success. Thus, although this approach does not blame potential entrants, it does require them to change to fit into a higher education that is developed to meet labour market needs. A transformative approach to widening participation, however, embraces the idea that higher education should change to meet the needs of students from under-represented groups and strive to benefit from greater diversity. Thus, the emphasis is on changing higher education systems and practices rather than moulding students to fit into a traditional, and perhaps inappropriate, form of HE. Such changes would include curricula and pedagogical developments and a more flexible higher education structure.

Drawing from our international study we proceed to explore ways in which national and regional governments and higher education systems are promoting the access and success of first generation entrants in higher education. National interventions include government-led targeting; data collection, evaluation and research; alternative admissions procedures; and alternative delivery. Institutional approaches include: pre-entry work; supporting students within interventions; and data collection and institutional research. Each of these types of interventions is illustrated with examples, considered in relation to underlying widening participation principles, and the potential benefits from first generation entrants are considered.

We conclude our book in Chapter 8 by drawing out what we feel to be the implications of our work for the future development of widening participation, in the UK and internationally. We argue that there is strong evidence for establishing first generation entrants as the key target group for widening participation policy and that this is the best way of ensuring that those who most need support will receive it. By targeting parental education those who experience double disadvantage, for example in respect of parental education and disability or ethnicity, can directly be reached. We reiterate that it is very difficult to disaggregate parental education from social class, but this does not mean they are entirely the same. If it were a choice between targeting parental education or socio-economic status, we would argue that parental education should be used, but ideally both should be considered together.

In terms of interventions, we argue that raising the aspirations of parents and families is not the issue. Parents want their children to have access to university opportunities that will sustain family harmony and promote family prosperity. Rather than trying to fit the family to the university, the university should focus on responding to the needs of the family. This means that assumptions cannot be made about insider knowledge of HE, and systems procedures and essential curriculum information should be transparent and understandable. On a deeper level it implies that a more flexible higher education needs to be developed.

The book concludes by outlining some future areas for research which will build on our multi-level international perspective and our interest in families. In particular it suggests that a focus on first generation entry might

bridge the current divide in educational research and practice between widening participation and informal and community based education. We end by calling for change at the both conceptual and material level in order to rethink widening participation to fully meet the needs of first generation entrants.

2

From a distance you can see more clearly: developing an international methodology with local benefits for student access and success

Introduction

The dramatic changes witnessed in tertiary education across the world prompt a need for international research on the new issues that now emerge, but undertaking such research effectively is not an easy matter. Novoa and Yariv-Mashal (2003) emphasize the importance of the ongoing debate about methodology in comparative research (see also Cowen 2000; Crossley 2002) and the need for: 'methodologies that do not consecrate models of analysis exclusively centred on national geographies and that are able to understand the multiplicity of affiliation and belonging that characterise communities across the world' (Novoa and Yariv-Mashal 2003; 433).

In order to undertake the international study on which we draw in this book, we needed to generate an appropriate methodology, which would allow us to engage with different national systems of higher education, undertake appropriate international analysis and produce benefits at a local level. In this chapter we discuss the methodological issues encountered in undertaking meaningful international comparative research, in particular the need for extended dialogue to explore definitions, meanings and interpretations *before* problems, priorities and solutions could be examined. The aim of the international comparative research study was to develop understanding about access and retention in tertiary education of under-represented groups, in order to assist national systems and education institutions to support these students to succeed. We sought to achieve this by challenging our own assumptions about problems, solutions and education systems and structures; theorizing the experiences of students from specific under-represented groups; and examining alternative policy solutions and interventions. As discussed in Chapter 1, the research brought together researchers from ten countries: Australia, Canada, Croatia, Germany, Ireland, Netherlands, Norway, Sweden, UK and US and involved a series of workshops, national reviews and an international comparative analysis.

The emphasis of the research was on the experience of students from

under-represented groups in tertiary education. The groups focused on are: low income or low socio-economic status groups; first generation entrants; minorities and refugees; students with disabilities; and mature students. These groups were identified by the research participants at the first research workshop (discussed below). First, it must be recognized that they are not necessarily homogeneous groups either in the way they are defined in different countries or within themselves (also discussed below). Second, individuals may fall into more than one of these equity groups and thus they are not discrete entities, and indeed the groupings may overlap and there may be similarities between them. Furthermore, each of these groups is not necessarily a priority in each country, which tends to impact on the data and research available; and there are other groups who are also important, and targeted in some countries, whom we did not include as an overall priority for our study.

As introduced in Chapter 1, we established an international network of researchers to take forward this and future international comparative work on student success. This research group has looked at the definitions of the target groups and the extent to which they are recognized and targeted; the availability of statistical data with regard to participation and retention of students from under-represented groups in the participating countries; existing research and understandings on the causes of failure, and research and practice supporting success; and the identification of gaps and key issues which need further investigation. It is hoped that further research will explore and test the 'critical success' factors identified in this initial study (Thomas and Quinn 2003a). The outputs of the first phase of the research include an International Retention Resource Bank, which includes an annotated bibliography; sources of relevant statistical information; details of academics and practitioners who are active in this field; useful websites and information about conferences and seminars; national reports on the access and success of students from the target groups in each of the participating countries; a research report synthesizing, analysing and presenting the research findings; and an international conference to promote further learning from this research project.

Undertaking international comparative research

The research study attempts to benefit from a global approach while also recognizing the importance of the local context (whether that is national, regional, local or individual). Globalization refers to '. . . those processes by which the peoples of the world are incorporated into a single society, global society' (Albrow and King 1990: 9), and such an approach recognizes that higher education worldwide is having to respond to 'a series of common challenges' (Eckel 2001: 103). Thus, in the context of this research a global perspective seeks to reduce the artificial significance of the nation state by

emphasizing the similarities between individuals and groups across boundaries. In other words, it seeks to explore the extent to which students from particular social or cultural groups have shared and different experiences in relation to participation in post-compulsory education.

There are, however, significant problems relating to undertaking international and comparative research in general, and particularly in relation to access and retention of students in tertiary education. Quantitative studies can present data about the participation of students from under-represented groups only *when* this data exists. In addition, there are methodological problems related to collating information from different national and institutional systems that use different definitions and reporting procedures. For example, OECD data on student retention and completion is of limited value as different national systems do not collect directly comparable data. Furthermore, statistical information is able to provide indicators of *trends*, but it does not provide insights into the complexity of the issues. Other studies avoid the difficulty of comparison by conducting coordinated research, but with limited comparative analysis (e.g. Schuetze and Slowey 2000; Osborne and Thomas 2003). Such an approach provides useful information about different national systems, but the interpretation is largely left to the reader. A final approach is to undertake comparative work with two or three countries thus minimizing the difficulties of comparing different systems and contexts.

When comparative work is undertaken there is a danger of reducing problems to the lowest common denominator, thus being unable to tackle the complexities of the issues and indulging in 'cherry picking' (McGrath 2001: 398) or the 'naive borrowing' (Evans et al. 1999: 2) of solutions which seem to work in another national context. Moreover, these solutions tend to be simplistic and inadequate ones because as Atkinson (2000) notes, ' "what works" is not enough'. Thus, McGrath comments: 'While this [interventionist solutions] allows the strengths of simplicity and certainty in the pronouncements produced, it is the failure to understand the systemic that fundamentally undermines the cherry-picking approach to comparativism both theoretically and practically' (McGrath 2001: 39). In a similar vein, Watson (1998) suggests that international and comparative research tends to ignore the 'temporal dynamics and contexts that help structure current realities and debates'. There are examples of effective comparative research, but these tend to be limited to two or three countries. Our international comparative research is much larger, involving ten countries, but it is committed to avoiding reducing the issues to a simplistic level. McGrath argues that an in situ understanding of the problem and solution is required, and thus he stresses the importance of the context, history and culture of both the problems encountered and the interventionist solutions presented, and the relevance of the national and local context is built into the research methodology. This point is of increasing importance as policy makers openly trawl for international examples of 'good practice' with a view to implementing them at home (see Galvin 2004).

Comparative work has its problems but so too does research on widening participation more generally. As researchers in this field, we are highly conscious of the dilemmas it currently faces. In many respects, research on access issues has been very parochial: tending to draw its conclusions from isolated institutional examples. Rather than adopting an analytical perspective, it is too often descriptive and even self-congratulatory, presenting uncritical accounts of initiatives and their success. These research accounts are rarely situated in that they are not reflexive about either researcher or method. Although theory does exist within the field (see, for example, Preece 1999) widening participation is, broadly speaking, under-theorized. There is a tendency to assume shared definitions, for example of what constitutes race or disability. Even more seriously, perhaps, there is assumption of shared values such as the desirability of access and the pernicious nature of drop out. Finally, in our opinion, there is a lack of methodological innovation and creativity, which needs to be addressed. This rather damning account is not the whole picture but it is a serious part of it. As researchers in widening participation we must necessarily include ourselves within it, as part of the problem as well as, we hope, part of the solution.

Our goal in progressing the international research was to generate 'situated knowledge' which countered the pitfalls of comparative and widening participation research outlined above. Drawing on Haraway (1988) we defined the characteristics of such knowledge as:

- Critical
- Reflexive
- Locatable – the site of knowledge can be identified and analysed
- Accountable
- Complex and Contradictory
- Generates webs of connections
- Looks both inward and outward

(Quinn 2002)

In this we are in accord with Novoa and Yariv-Mashal who argue that the focus of comparative research should not be 'facts or 'realities' but 'problems':

> ... problems that are located and relocated in places and times ... problems that can only be elucidated through the adoption of new *zones of looking* that are inscribed in a space delineated by frontiers of meaning and not only by physical boundaries.

(2003: 437)

Methods developed and used

In order to avoid 'naive borrowing' or 'cherry picking' from a set of disconnected national examples of good practice we attempted to design a fully

comparative and cross-national analysis which grew from local understandings. The methodology employed draws on the comparative work of Evans et al. (1999) in the field of post-compulsory education and training. Evans et al. advocate a process of mutual learning and multi-layering. Mutual learning puts dialogue at the heart of the research process, as it is through interaction that an in depth understanding is developed. This, for example, helps to safeguard against naive borrowing, as problems and policy solutions are not taken out of context, but rather a two way process of understanding and learning is engaged in. Evans et al. write that mutual learning '. . . is an essential feature, allowing discourse on cases and discourse on variables to develop into extended dialogues between ideas and evidence' (Evans et al. 1999: 1). Such an approach draws on the contextualized knowledge and lived experiences of local, or 'indigenous', researchers who are 'the pivots between the insider views and the wider discourses' (Evans et al. 1999: 10). Multi-layering is the process of looking at different perspectives, in this case different policy levels, such as policy as espoused, policy as enacted and policy as experienced. Thus, the experience is not limited to the national level but also takes account of the local sphere, the institutional arena and the experience of individual students. The next section discusses how the processes of mutual learning and multi-layering have been operationalized within our research study.

Mutual learning has been achieved by a participative approach involving research practitioners from each of the participating countries as equal partners in research workshops and the preparation of national reports. Each of the research participants was invited to join the research group, but this was based on a known or expressed interest in the issues of access and success of students from under-represented groups. This voluntary participation has resulted in members having a genuine interest in the research topics, and this is usually related to their professional role. This has helped to ensure that people are committed to the research and are willing to engage in a process of mutual learning, which challenges their own assumptions and operating norms. The process may at times be uncomfortable, but overall it is very rewarding. The participants are not all in the same role in their own countries: some are employed by education institutions (as researchers, lecturers, support staff and managers/administrators), others work for government agencies, or in campaigning organizations. Furthermore, individuals have particular areas of interest and expertise. Rather than being problematic, this tends to enhance the mutual learning process as a wider range of discussion occurs, and facilitates multi-layering as people relate more directly to different levels. Thus, not only are a range of countries and institutions represented in our research team but so too are different interest groups and different levels and roles within the intervention process. Each individual has areas of expertise and knowledge, and areas where they are less well informed, but this combination makes for a strengthened research team.

The research workshops have contributed to the process of mutual

learning by developing understanding through dialogue and discussion about the key issues. The first of these was devoted to discussing the parameters of the research, and explored the questions, 'What do we mean by "higher", "post-secondary" or "post-compulsory" education?' 'What terms do we use for early withdrawal, and what do they mean?' and, 'What are the priority issues and groups in each country?' This process helped to frame the research context, issues and questions, and informed the preparation of the research proposal. Furthermore, this approach helped to ensure that the research project was relevant to all of the research partners.

A second function of the day was to explore the information we wanted to collect. This process was continued at the second research meeting. Some partners brought along and shared information about data and policies to support student success in their own country. This led to discussions, not only about the information being presented, but more importantly about the similarities and differences with other systems and the underlying assumptions that informed these systems. From a methodological perspective this helped to identify the questions that we needed to ask of ourselves for the research to progress, and a clear structure for the national reports (discussed below) was created.

For the third research workshop all participants were asked to prepare and circulate national reports. The focus was on sharing and analysing the material from different countries, and relating it back to participants' own experiences and contexts. The national reports were circulated in advance, but the emphasis was on actively reflecting on your own national situation in light of the learning from other countries, rather than passively listening to the problems and solutions of others. Thus participants reflected on and discussed what they had learnt about their own system, such as areas where no data was available, particular priority issues, those that are not perceived to be significant and why and also identified questions that had been raised. Bi- or tri-lateral comparative analysis was undertaken in small groups to start identifying similarities, differences and questions where more information is required. This was supplemented by an initial analysis in relation to each of the target groups at three levels (system, institution and individual). The whole process took place over two days, and following this third research workshop it was agreed that each of the national reports would be revised to clarify issues and add in additional information as appropriate.

The final research workshop focused on interpretation. Initial findings from the analysis of the revised research reports were presented to the group and discussed. Participants questioned and corrected interpretations, clarified and added information and provided further examples to illustrate the findings.

National reports have also been used to help promote mutual learning. In part, by facilitating researchers to develop their own understanding by reflecting on their national and institutional contexts in order to make their own experiences intelligible and meaningful to co-researchers from other countries. Simultaneously, the process has produced information to assist

the research team as a whole to learn about issues from alternative perspectives, and to challenge our own underpinning assumptions about issues such as data collection, labelling, barriers to success and strategies to address these issues. The national reports capture data about the education system as a whole, as well as about the tertiary system. Initially this process was quite unstructured, but it became apparent through discussion that national operating norms would not necessarily be perceived as worthy of description as they were taken for granted knowledge. It was through reading the reports and further dialogue that it became apparent that a more structured approach was required, and this was facilitated by the generation of a list of 24 questions about the national education system. In addition, the national reports included descriptive and statistical data about access to and success in tertiary education by the target groups, research data about these issues and policy approaches and interventions.

Preparing and researching the national reports provided members of the research team with an opportunity for self-reflection. In particular, participants felt that this process revealed the complexity of their own national system and helped foster a clearer understanding of how that system worked, by providing new perspectives and challenging underlying assumptions. For example, in relation to data sources, participants identified and compared fragmented national data sources as well as looking at data at a range of levels. This revealed a lack of coherence of data sources *within* countries and gaps in the data. When these issues were discussed different cultural norms regarding data collection were discovered, such as what was acceptable and what was not. For example certain questions about ethnic origin now routinely used in the UK were considered impermissible in a Swedish or Norwegian context. In addition, some common problems regarding the availability of 'sensitive data' emerged, particularly in the context of disability, where no 'true' picture was felt to exist anywhere because of the various incentives and disadvantages of self-disclosure. However, there was a useful process of sharing data collection tools and participants believed that they could identify some relevant data, perhaps using indirect approaches to data collection. It was also acknowledged that knowing the gaps in the data is equally important. Furthermore, the discussion about the data revealed potentially similar trends between countries in relation to target groups: for example, those from lower socio-economic groups have low participation rates in HE in all ten countries in comparison to the majority of the population.

With regard to multi-layering, it was apparent from the beginning of the research project that it was necessary to take into account different levels of intervention, in particular, national systems, states or regions, institutions, academic disciplines and individual student experiences. This approach is essential for two reasons. First, different systems exist in the participating countries, which provide different emphases on the level of intervention. For example, Australia has a unified national system of higher education, with prescribed equity groups and standard definitions and a comprehensive

national data collection procedure. This can be contrasted with countries such as Canada, Germany and the US, where the role of the Federal government is significantly less. In Canada for example, there is little national intervention, but regional and institutional policies are highly influential. A second reason for a multi-layered approach is that target groups will be subject to different espoused, enacted and experienced policies, thus it is important not just to look at what interventions are planned, but how they are implemented and the impact on student groups. In our ten country international project we have relied on the analysis of secondary data, rather than undertaking new empirical work, but by utilizing a broad range of information, such as national, regional and institutional policies and practices, published and grey literature, statistical data and existing empirical research from each of the participating countries we have been able to explore interventions at different levels. By linking our international project to our empirical qualitative project on drop out, which also has an international dimension, we have been able to focus down on the texture of the lives of first generation students (see Chapters 4 and 6) and thus add a further dimension to the book.

Within the international project, building on the workshop discussions, the national reports and associated literature, we proceeded to develop a comparative analysis across the ten countries. This was thematically framed around the target groups and was ultimately produced as and presented to an international audience in Amsterdam (Thomas and Quinn 2003a). Our role within the project was to act as initiators, facilitators of discussion, coordinators of information, analysts of data and ultimately communicators of the joint project. We do not however see ourselves as 'owners' of the project. Members of the research team have used the work in their negotiations with policy makers and institutions and in developing further research projects in their own countries as well as maintaining diverse links with us.

Our relationship with the project can also be seen as methodologically challenging. As demonstrated in the foregoing discussion, the concepts, approaches and understandings were participatively developed with the research team, who helped us to reach a point where we could begin to comprehend and work with data from ten very different countries. Without this grounding it would have been futile to begin this task. However, without the research hub which we provided it would have been impossible for the project to function or to move beyond the simple accumulation or synthesis of information. With the financial support of the Sutton Trust and the Esmée Fairbairn Foundation we were able to dedicate the time and expertise to pull together, compare and provide a critical analysis of the data. It is this critical analysis that informs our book.

In summary, the research methodology used has sought to make further use of the policies and practices, data and research from ten countries, while guarding against the charge of cherry picking or naive borrowing, which at best will have limited results. We have drawn from the work of Evans et al. (1999) (mutual learning and multi-layering) and developed a research

methodology with three distinctive features: utilizing and prioritizing the knowledge of practitioner-researchers from the participating countries; research workshops to promote dialogue; and the preparation of structured national reports to assist self-discovery and to facilitate comparative learning and ultimately a comparative analysis across the ten countries. The next section details some of the dilemmas we faced in undertaking international comparative research, and the ways in which this methodological approach assisted in resolving them.

Developing a common language

International dialogue is at the heart of this research process and therefore developing a commonly understood language is crucial. Although English is the language of exchange there are far more complex communication issues with regard to definitions, meanings and interpretations before we can start to explore problems, priorities and solutions. In the early stages of the research three key questions were central to our project, 'What is higher education?' 'How is retention defined?' and, 'Who are the target groups?' The answers to these questions formed the boundaries for our research, and thus it was important to challenge and explore these at the early stages of our study, as once a course has been plotted it can be difficult to change direction (Blackmore and Ison 1998). Each of these issues is discussed below.

What is higher education?

In order to create a boundary around the research field we needed to consider the question, 'What is higher education?' This question stimulated discussion about the types of institutions and courses which should and should not be included in our research. Following extended discussion we opted to use the definitions drawn up by the OECD (1999). Initially, we adopted the International Standard Classification of Education (ISCED) Tertiary A definition, which accords with more traditional, academically oriented provision. However, comments at an international conference and subsequent reflection by the research team suggested that this approach was incorrect as it would exclude large numbers of widening participation students who are engaged in less traditional programmes of study. Thus we also included 5b, which is closely allied with professional and vocational qualifications and includes shorter, two-year programmes. The key features of ISCED 5 are:

- Programmes have an educational content more advanced than those offered at Levels 3 (upper-secondary level) and 4 (post-secondary, non-tertiary).
- Entry to these programmes normally requires the successful completion

of an upper secondary qualification or a similar post-secondary non-tertiary qualification.

• Programmes at Level 5 must have a cumulative theoretical duration of at least two years from the beginning of Level 5 and do not lead directly to the award of an advanced research qualification (those programmes are at Level 6).

Adopting these OECD definitions made drawing the research boundaries relatively straightforward, although it was more difficult when it came to putting the investigation into practice. For example, in Australia some courses delivered in the vocational education and training (VET) sector are categorized as 5b programmes, while others are ISCED-4 (for example, shorter training courses) but the data and research is not always disaggregated in this way. However, the general focus of the research project is on *tertiary education* (OECD 1999), and different types of tertiary education were differentiated in the national reports and the discussions below as appropriate. In this book we have chosen to focus on first generation entrants studying for degrees within universities (5a) and are using the data from our project that particularly apply to such courses (OECD 1999).

What is student retention?

A crucial question to address is, 'What is student retention?' Even posing this question is problematic, as the term used presupposes the answer to some extent. However, the research team began by identifying terms which are widely used by students to refer to staying and completing their initial tertiary education programme within an acceptable time frame, and those used when students do not conform to this norm. In all approximately 20 terms were identified, but what is important to note is the different implications that these terms carry with them. For example, some expressions individualize and place responsibility on the students, for example, 'persistence', 'withdrawal' and 'student success'; while others operate at the level of the system and thus the responsibility is shifted to the institution or the government, for example, 'retention' and 'graduation rates'. Some phrases, such as 'drop out' and 'failure' (rate) carry with them blame, while others emphasize choice, for example, 'student mobility' and 'stop out'. The research team felt that 'student success' and 'student mobility' were more positive terms than the others, but 'retention' was selected as the preferred generic term, as it emphasizes systemic responsibility; it was also familiar and widely understood (in part due to its prevalence in US literature).

It must be acknowledged, however, that terms do have specific technical meanings in different countries and the context informs their usage, thus one cannot simply use 'retention' in all circumstances. For example, in Sweden the 'retention rate' refers to the number of new entrants who are registered as students after one year including those who have transferred to

another institution, while 'graduation rates' include those who have completed their higher education course and those who leave the system with three or more years of documented education. Thus each of these terms has a technical definition and the cultural context shapes the definition. In Sweden, for example, students are able to move between institutions, data is collected nationally and so movement is captured, and leaving tertiary education without having completed a target qualification is valued rather than perceived as a failure. Consequently, retention is used as the dominant generic term in this research, but more precise terms are defined and used when appropriate.

Who are the target groups?

This question can be interpreted in two ways: 'Who are the target groups in relation to this research project?' and, 'How are they defined?' Agreeing the target groups for this research project was surprisingly unproblematic. At the first research meeting four target groups were identified and agreed upon: first generation entrants; students from low socio-economic groups (SEGs) or low income families; students from ethnic minority/foreign backgrounds; and students with disabilities. Two key issues should be noted however. First, these groups are more or less important in different countries. For example, in countries where students with disabilities have long been included in tertiary education as a result of a culture of inclusion, robust legislation and financial support for institutions, this topic is generally of little interest. Conversely, in a country like Croatia with a comparatively high level of disability and more recent interest in actively including these students in tertiary education, this is an area of great importance. An interesting sub-group is that of 'refugees', who were included within the target groups by the research team but who do not feature highly in any country's approach to equity in tertiary education. The second point to note is that there are other target groups. For example, in Norway there is considerable policy interest and research regarding the participation of women in tertiary education and in particular disciplines. In Australia populations in rural and isolated areas are a targeted equity group, which is largely a consequence of the geographical landscape of the country. In four countries participating in the research there are indigenous populations that are largely underrepresented in tertiary education. These are not the focus of this research, but information has been utilized where appropriate. Adult or mature students are an important group in some countries, for example, they were an early focus of the access movement in the UK (access courses and qualifications now being synonymous with students over the age of 21), but in other countries the age of students is of little concern. In Ireland there is a dearth of older students (over 23) in tertiary education and thus it was felt that it would be useful to include mature age students, to explore their participation and retention rates.

The issue of how particular target groups are defined is central to the research process and findings. It is by examining different definitions that assumptions about the barriers to success become apparent, and these in turn shape the subsequent policy prescriptions and interventions. Equally, some categorizations omit key issues which inhibit retention and success, and thus help to explain lower rates of success in tertiary education. The next section explores some of these findings from the research to illustrate the value of this methodological approach.

Creating new understandings

One of the outcomes of our research was to problematize the definitions of target groups used within widening participation by acknowledging and working with the flexibility of 'local' categories as found across the ten countries. (see the Conclusion of this chapter) There are, however, significant difficulties associated with defining and comparing information when there are no uniform categories. Therefore, a significant part of this research is focused on the different classifications that are used. The analysis of these definitions has provided further insight into the issues of access and retention of students from under-represented groups. Embedded in the national categories and understandings are assumptions which inform the policy solutions. Deconstructing these meanings and exploring alternative constructions can assist us to question our own implicit underlying values, expand our understanding of the issues, suggest alternative ways of responding to the issues and provide contextual understanding to assist international learning. In a similar vein, Evans et al. (1999) comment:

> The overall purposes are for research participants to gain new perspectives and insights, to understand issues and practices in their own system better, to evaluate the need, scope and the prospects of success for particular changes; to anticipate effects and unintended consequences; and to counter naive 'borrowing' by understanding the macro forces and factors which create or limit the possibilities for change
>
> (Evans et al. 1999: 2)

This point can be illustrated by an example. The research has identified three distinct ways of categorizing minority groups: place of birth; language; and racial or ethnic group. Each of these ways of defining minority groups emphasizes different shared characteristics, but equally brings together people with very different histories, and the underlying assumptions frame the solutions adopted. These different foci (national background, linguistic difference and racial/ethnic identity) prioritize or draw attention to particular barriers to access and progression in tertiary education. 'Place of birth' or 'country of origin' is related to knowledge of the education system, and in some conceptualizations, such as that of the German *Bildungsinländer*, experience of the education and qualifications

system. Linguistic difference clearly prioritizes language difficulties while racial or ethnic group emphasizes the cultural differences and discrimination. In the UK we only consider ethnic background and ignore the differences in problems faced by students who are newly arrived to the UK as opposed to those faced by students who have been born and brought up here for one or more generations, and we do not identify or track the experiences of minority groups for whom English is not their first language. These insights help clarify the assumptions underpinning higher education policies (Thomas 2001) and suggest that a more sophisticated definition would improve targeting and support for minority students in tertiary education in the UK. For instance, Australia combines linguistic background with place of birth (length of time in the country); and the Netherlands prioritizes place of birth, and within this category specific ethnic minorities are identified and targeted.

In most countries, defining 'mature' students appears to be far less problematic, as it is based on age. But it is interesting to note that the national age of mature students varies from 21 in the UK to 25 in Australia, Sweden and Norway (23 in Ireland, 24 in the US), and countries such as the Netherlands and Croatia do not have a defined age. Only in Canada has defining mature students caused significant national debate, and in Germany age is not considered, but rather educational entry qualifications. A closer discussion of these different ages and the assumptions under-pinning them reveals that although initially age appears to be the defining feature of mature students, in most cases it is being used as a short-hand or proxy for other characteristics, which are usually not explicit. These can be summarized as: financial dependence or independence; traditional entry qualification or educational disadvantage; direct entrance from school or work experience and mode of study; full or part time, or distance learning (which may relate to additional dependants and commitments). A definition of mature students, or 'second chance students' which made explicit some or all of these characteristics would seem more useful to facilitate an effective targeting and provision of support to help ensure student success. Currently all mature students tend to be lumped together on the basis of age, but in reality they may face very different barriers to access and success.

The research also considered alternative conceptualizations of socio-economic status, which was influential in relation to the preparation of this book. We therefore discuss the different ways in which lower socio-economic status is defined, and the implications of this, in more detail in Chapter 4.

The local benefits of international research

We have found that developing such a truly international perspective has many benefits for a researcher. First, it removes you from the particularities and self-protections of your own institution: for when working at a solely institutional level there are many things you cannot see; things you do not

want to see; and those that others do not want you to see. It also removes you from national policy imperatives, where research at a national level is driven by what is currently deemed important. However, it does not leave you floating, but rather forces you to explain and clarify your own position to others and to re-examine and question this position. In terms of our own work, it has freed us up in some significant ways. It has allowed us to return to key questions such as why 'class' remains so central to widening participation internationally. It has allowed us to glimpse and explore new possibilities such as the fully integrated student databases in Sweden. New strategies emerge from unexpected quarters like the emphasis on systematic student centred evaluation of teaching and learning in Croatia. Heretical positions are permitted such as the explicit targeting of equity groups in Australia. Most importantly, all these cases can be critically understood rather than unquestioningly appropriated. We also now know far more about our own relative national strengths and weaknesses: for example, while provision for mature students is comparatively well developed in the UK, retention of lower socio-economic groups is comparatively poor.

Having been active in an international project we have found that internationalism has become part of our way of approaching research and that we now routinely integrate international perspectives within UK based research projects. One such example is the Joseph Rowntree Foundation project discussed in this book (see Chapters 4 and 6), where members of the international retention research team were commissioned to write papers on how drop out was perceived and addressed in their own countries, and were supported to present and address these papers at an international colloquium on the project's interim findings. Having this broader vision helped us to challenge the dominance of the rhetoric of retention in the UK and envisage a much more flexible lifelong learning Higher Education system (see Quinn et al. 2005).

Although the international research has offered us a privileged escape from the local and the contingent, there are many practical ways in which its lessons can be brought back home. The remainder of this book seeks to share some of these new insights, particularly in relation to first generation entry.

Conclusions

This research project sought to undertake an international comparative study in which policies, practices, research and data from different countries were utilized to improve understandings about access and retention of students from under-represented groups, and to inform policies and practices at all levels of intervention. The research team, however, is wary of the technical limitations of international comparative analysis (for example not being able to compare 'like with like') and the social, economic, political, cultural and historical factors that impinge on the direct transfer of interventions

and strategies from one context to another. We have sought to produce situated knowledge which avoids the pitfalls of much international research and the shortcomings of work on widening participation more generally. To this end we have utilized, adapted and developed Evans et al. (1999) methodological approach based on mutual learning and multi-layering. In particular, the importance of extended dialogue through research workshops has been discussed, and the use of a structured approach to the collection of national information from indigenous researchers, for whom norms and values are implicit and thus need to be 'extracted'. The importance of boundary setting has been highlighted, but there are inherent difficulties in doing this as countries use different understandings and definitions to inform their policies, practices, data collection and research. The use of OECD definitions of tertiary education has helped to minimize the problem, although some definitional issues cannot be overcome. However, this research approach has seen difference as a strength to be utilized, rather than as a weakness to be overcome: the analysis has made use of these differences to deconstruct the meanings underpinning labels and extend our understanding of the issues. This process of deconstruction and analysis helps to clarify the various barriers to access, retention and success, and to inform strategies to improve them – which is the overall goal of this research project. The distancing and 'making strange' involved in developing a truly international perspective has enabled us to see more clearly what needs to be done when we get 'back home'. We hope that this research strategy and this book will assist readers to start seeing things differently and to question some implicit assumptions in their own work.

3

The access and success of students from lower socio-economic groups in higher education

Introduction

This chapter considers the access and success of students from lower socio-economic groups in an international context. The chapter begins by analysing international documents to uncover how 'lower socio-economic groups' and first generation entrants are defined and operationalised in different countries and contexts. It then reviews the access and success of these targeted groups in the countries involved in our study. Of particular significance is the fact that students from lower socio-economic groups are identified and targeted in each of the participating countries as their participation is lower than the majority. However, students from lower socio-economic groups do not have lower rates of 'success' (however this is defined) in all participating countries. This suggests that it is not inevitable that a higher proportion of non-traditional students will 'fail' compared to their peers, but rather that different education systems may support these students better than others.

What do we mean by 'lower socio-economic groups'?

The international research team identified a number of broad types of under-represented groups to be the focus of the study (see Chapter 1). This included 'students from lower socio-economic groups', but discussion quickly revealed that this broad categorization is defined differently in each of the participating countries. The definitions of 'lower socio-economic status' vary considerably and reflect the ways in which society and the education system are constructed and conceptualized. The four main factors determining or contributing to low economic status that the international study identified were: income, occupation, geography and parental level of education. The following discussion shows how these factors are used in exemplar countries and the implications this has for the interventions that are put in place.

Income

One approach to defining 'lower socio-economic status' is to use either the student's or their family's income. These figures can then be related to participation rates in higher education. The most explicit example is in the US, where up to the age of 24 a student's parental income is used, and beyond this age the student's own income is taken into account instead. Studies in the US measure income and relate this to HE participation, including rates of access, where students study, completion rates and duration of study.

Longitudinal studies in the US show that consistently students from the lowest income quartile are under-represented in higher education (see Mortenson 2005), and indeed the situation is worsening. For more details see: *The Forgotten Half Revisited* (1998); *Access Denied: Restoring the Nation's Commitment to Equal Opportunity* (2000); and *Empty Promises: The Myth of College Access in America* (2002). Income is also used to examine where students participate in higher education (in other words, which institutions and institutional types), and their rates of success (completion and duration). Although a factor in the debate may be to do with issues of academic preparedness, even well prepared low income students are less likely to participate in HE. Allen et al. (2005) have shown that in the US the best prepared low income students go to higher education at the same rate as the worst prepared richer students (around 78 percent) – whereas the worst prepared low income students are only entering HE at a rate of around 36 percent.

In the US institutions set their own fees, which are influenced by the market, their mission and institutional type (private or public university, as the latter usually receives a state subsidy, or community college). In addition, institutions offer financial support to students – including the discounting of tuition and fees – in varying degrees, reflecting the complex interplay of cost, academic selectivity, recruitment pool and efforts to achieve equity and diversity. Poorer students are more strongly influenced by cost than other students, and the US league tables show a sharp divergence in student profile depending on institutional reputation, academic selectivity and other factors. Public institutions are generally lower cost than private ones, especially for students who study in-state; this creates a powerful incentive for poorer students to study locally. Community colleges provide an even more local, and even cheaper alternative. They provide the option for students to study the first two years of higher education, either to achieve a two year associate degree, or to then transfer into a four year bachelor degree programme at a university. Community college students are more likely to be low income and minority ethnic – and their courses are cheaper. Many of these students transfer to a university to complete a bachelor degree.

The mobility and flexibility in the US HE system means that students change courses and institutions frequently. On average students change their major (degree subject) five times, and they often attend more than one institution – some times at the same time – which is known as 'swirling'. Department of Education figures show that typically a student will attend

more than one institution to earn a degree (US Department of Education 2002). This flexibility has an impact on duration of study, and the poorer you are the longer you are likely to take to graduate.

Income is related to attainment too. In 1975 around 7 percent of all those from the bottom income quartile gained a baccalaureate degree by age 24, and 40 percent of those in the top quartile, in 2000 the percentage for the low income quartile had remained constant while that in the top quartile had risen above 60 percent (Allen et al. 2005).

The US approach to equitable access to higher education can be characterized as one that seeks to enable individual students to go to college, primarily by ensuring that the financial barriers are not unduly high. Although there has been a vigorous debate about affirmative action in terms of race, the main focus is on assistance to the individual student rather than a requirement for institutional action or change. There is a federal outreach programme – TRIO – and outreach activity at the institutional level, but the major focus of endeavour is on financial support. There is less focus on subsequent attainment and student success in terms of equity per se.

Student financial support is composed of federal, state and institutional aid, as well as family contributions. Federal assistance includes means tested Pell Grants, loans and education tax credits. State financial aid, can include need-based grants, merit-based scholarships, loans and/or subsidized provision (in other words, public institutions for in-state students). Institutional financial aid may include need-based and merit-based support in the form of grants or loans, discounted fees, and other forms of support such as campus employment. If the family is unable to provide sufficient additional financial support, private sector loans and other forms of private borrowing such as credit card debt may be incurred.

The principal grant targeted to low income students is the federal Pell Grant, which is a means tested grant for students from families typically with an annual income below US$25,000. The Higher Education Act of 1965 targeted the Basic Educational Opportunity Grants (BEOG), later renamed Pell Grants, to students, particularly low income students, rather than institutions. By doing this Congress went some way toward ensuring that cost as a barrier to HE should be minimized, and that there should be some degree of choice between public and private institutions. The maximum funded Pell grant currently stands at just over US$4,000 per annum. Increasingly, however, the bulk of federal support is provided through loans, both subsidized and unsubsidized, and through tax credits, which are available to middle income, as well as low income, families.

In addition, almost all states in the US have means tested financial assistance programmes. For example, in Illinois the state grant is called the Monetary Award Program (MAP); this has a maximum award of about US$4,500 per annum. However, state financial aid schemes vary widely. It is instructive to note that today 80 percent of the total volume of state financial aid comes from five states: Illinois, Pennsylvania, New York, New Jersey and California; thus students' access to state financial aid is highly dependent on

where they live. Furthermore, States can select the type of aid they wish to provide and thus prioritize which students they support. Thus, college participation rates vary widely by region and state. In particular, low income college participation rates range from a high of over 40 percent in states such as Minnesota, New Hampshire and New Jersey, to lows of under 20 percent in Alabama, Arizona, Arkansas and New Mexico (Conklin and Wellner 2004).

US institutions provide financial aid of different types: need-based and merit-based grants and loans, discounted fees (perhaps up to 30 percent), and campus employment. The level and type of support varies significantly depending on an institution's financial and market position, and its mission. Once the need of a student has been calculated, the financial aid office at the student's institution prepares a financial aid package to meet as much of this need as possible, through federal grants and loans (if eligible) plus work–study arrangements and institutional grants. Currently about 70 percent of American college students receive some sort of financial aid in this manner, a proportion that has increased over time as college costs have risen.

In addition to financial aid, activities to widen participation tend to focus on outreach activity to encourage aspiration and access. At the national level there is funding to support some of this activity via TRIO – a set of programmes designed to complement federal financial aid. By law, the programmes are targeted to low income and first generation students, where low income is defined as 150 percent of poverty level (currently, about US$28,000 in net taxable income for a family of four), and where first generation is defined as neither parent having completed a bachelor's degree. The original three TRIO programmes, set up in the 1960s were focused on improving access, facilitating the transition to higher education, and increasing college-based retention (defined as baccalaureate completion). Today there are eight TRIO programmes serving over 850,000 low income students across the country – six of which are targeted directly at students and would-be students, and two of which deal with training for TRIO staff and dissemination of successful programmes to institutions and agencies that do not have TRIO grants. TRIO funds are awarded to institutions through competitive grant funding. Studies have shown that students in the Upward Bound programme are four times more likely to earn an undergraduate degree than those students from similar backgrounds who did not participate in TRIO; and nearly 20 percent of all Black and Hispanic freshmen who entered college in 1981 received assistance through the TRIO Talent Search or the Educational opportunity Centers. However, only one in four American colleges and universities houses a TRIO programme, and the Council For Opportunity in Education (the professional organization for TRIO staff) estimates that the programmes reach only 7 percent of the low income Americans eligible to be served.

In summary, student or family income level is a straight forward way of defining socio-economic status. Assuming the data are available, it is a less ambiguous way than some of the other approaches to delineating

socio-economic status. However, as the example of the US demonstrates, defining students in this way emphasizes their access to finance – which is undoubtedly an important issue in relation to entry to and success in higher education – but is less able to address some of the other potential challenges that students and their families face (see Chapters 5 and 6).

Occupation

A number of countries, such as Canada, Germany, Ireland and the UK use the occupation of a student or their parents as an indicator of socio-economic status. For example in Canada the Blishen socio-economic index for fathers' occupations when respondents were 15 years old is used. Young people are then classified into three socio-economic groups: those who fall into the highest quartiles of the Blishen index; those who fall into the middle half and those who fall into the lowest quartile. This Blishen Index is over 20 years old and ignores the contribution that women make to families – through income and employment background. Implicit in employment definitions, at least traditionally, is family income and occupational status (which may relate to parental education).

Data from Canada (see Table 3.1) shows how young people from the lower socio-economic groups (according to the Blishen Index) are persistently under-represented in university education. In 1986 14 percent of young people (18–21) from the lowest socio-economic groups participated in university education, compared with 33 percent of young people from the highest socio-economic groups. By 1998 the position had improved somewhat, but a significant gap in participation rates remained: 18.5 percent of young people from the lowest socio-economic groups participated, and 38.5 percent from the highest socio-economic groups. During the same time period the gap between the middle socio-economic groups and the highest narrowed. Similar patterns, favouring students from professional families, can be seen in other countries that base their socio-economic indicators on employment.

This raises the key question of how these countries seek to improve the access and success of students from lower socio-economic groups. An important approach to widening access to higher education in Canada

Table 3.1   University participation rate of 18–21-year-olds by socio-economic status of family in Canada

	Lowest SEGs (%)	*Middle SEGs (%)*	*Highest SEGs (%)*
1986	14.0	15.0	33.0
1994	18.0	25.0	40.0
1998	18.5	27.5	38.5

Source: Chenard and Bonin (2003)

is the Canada Millennium Scholarship Foundation, established by an Act of Parliament in 1998 with an endowment of C\$2.5 billion. The aim of the Foundation is to help Canadians meet the challenges of a rapidly changing economy and society by creating opportunities for them to pursue post-secondary education. It creates:

- Opportunities to learn, by providing financial assistance to students and by piloting new ways to improve access to post-secondary education;
- Opportunities to grow, by challenging students to make a difference in their schools and in their communities by assisting them in developing their longer term goals; and
- Opportunities to contribute, by challenging all Canadians to ensure that Canada's students are equipped to meet the challenges of a new millennium.

However, 95 percent of the Foundation's endowment is used to provide bursaries to post-secondary students.

In Ireland, there is a similar focus on financial support to widen access in third level education (Thornhill 2002). This includes no fees for under-graduate programmes for all students, a modest means tested grant, and the Disadvantaged Fund, consisting of the Student Assistance Access Fund and the Special Fund for Students with Disabilities. Further financial support is provided by the European Social Fund for 'disadvantaged' and disabled students. Other strategies include a focus on policy development (as recommended by Skilbeck and Connell 2000; Osborne and Leith 2000), research and publications.

The Irish Higher Education Authority also implemented a Targeted Initiatives Programme, which is intended to increase the participation of disadvantaged school leavers, mature students and students who have a disability. Rather than being influenced by the financial disadvantages of students from lower socio-economic groups, the Report of the Steering Group on the Future of Higher Education (1995, see Carpenter 2003) identified three key aspects of socio-economic inequality in relation to entry to higher education. These were that students from lower socio-economic groups are significantly less likely complete second level (high school) education, those that sit the Leaving Certificate tend to achieve significantly lower grades and for students with modest levels of performance in the Leaving Certificate those from higher socio-economic groups have a higher transfer rate to higher education. The Report argued that Targeted Initiatives should focus on these three areas to increase the representation of those from lower socio-economic groups (Carpenter 2003). Targeted Initiatives include a wide range of interventions that address information, experiential and educational gaps that students from lower socio-economic groups may experience, for example, links with schools, residentials at higher education institutions, mentoring schemes, supervised study and supplementary tuition, direct entry arrangements, programmes for parents, guidance counselling and orientation programmes (Thornhill 2002).

Socio-economic status indicators based on employment can offer a broader approach to widening access and success in higher education. In Canada, however, using employment to define socio-economic status has led to an emphasis on the lack of economic capital that students from these families have access to. This approach largely ignores the importance of other types of capital, such as cultural and social capital. However, in Ireland, some interventions have focused on financial issues, while research has led to a recognition of the other factors that impact on the access of students from lower socio-economic groups, thus institutional level interventions address educational achievement in secondary school and lack of awareness and information about higher education by students and their families. It should be noted however that using employment as an indicator of socio-economic status does not directly draw attention to the disparities in social and cultural capital that students have access to. Furthermore, the emphasis appears to be to equip students to enter higher education, whether through financial support, school achievement or improving progression opportunities, rather than considering how these students fare within higher education.

Geography

An approach to defining socio-economic status that has become more explicit in recent years is geography – or rather where people live and what this signifies. In both Australia and the UK geographical areas are used to identify under-represented groups on the basis of lifestyle opportunities, choices and values. In Australia low socio-economic status is a target group for widening participation, and it is based on where people live. In the UK higher education institutions are paid a 'post code premium' to support the recruitment and retention of students from homes with postcodes associated with low rates of participation. There is an implicit link between location and income, but this approach seeks to include an element of choice or taste reflected in the decisions people make about where they live.

Australia has had a higher education fees contribution scheme for undergraduate courses (HECS) since 1989. This policy change was accompanied by the publication of *A Fair Chance for All: Education That's Within Everyone's Reach* in 1990 by the Commonwealth Government (see DEET 1990). Although this document is over 15 years old now, it continues to shape most equity activity. The document identified and designated as disadvantaged six groups on the basis of their under-representation in the higher education student population (see DEET 1990: appendix 1). This includes 'people from socio-economically disadvantaged backgrounds', who are defined as 'residents in an area with low socio-economic status as a surrogate for students' low socio-economic status'. In relation to each equity category, institutional data is used to construct indicators for the access, participation, success and retention of these students in comparison with other students. This information is collected nationally and used to monitor the performance

of the higher education system as a whole in achieving national equity targets. Individual institutions use the indicators to monitor the progress towards the equity targets that they set themselves and to compare their performance with that of other institutions (Ferrier and Heagney 2001). A similar approach, based on the Australian model, has been developed and adopted in the UK (Tonks 1999).

What kind of interventions does a geographical approach to defining socio-economic status give rise to? In Australia further changes to higher education were introduced in December 2004; these include partial deregulation of fees for all subjects, except education and nursing, graduates of which are in short supply. This has been accompanied by a number of initiatives to provide financial support. These include the FEEHelp scheme which offers low interest loans, and Commonwealth government scholarships which are allocated on the basis of post code analysis. At the institutional level the emphasis has been on outreach with schools in low participation neighbourhoods, and other similar interventions to encourage these students to enter higher education.

In the UK the use of geography or location to categorize students from lower socio-economic groups has focused widening access interventions on the development of regional approaches. In England this is exemplified by Aimhiger, in Scotland by the four regional forums (sic) and in Wales Reaching Higher Reaching Wider has adopted a similar regional approach. These initiatives tend to work with schools with low rates of either achievement at 16 (e.g. five GCSEs or more, grade A–C) or progression to post-16 and/or higher education. The emphasis is on raising the awareness of young people about higher education and that it is a realistic opportunity for them, improving educational achievement in school (usually indirectly by improving motivation) and the provision of information, advice and guidance to support entry to higher education.

The focus on geography seems to recognize both income and educational experience to some extent. Income is likely to restrict where people live, but this may be further influenced by taste and choices. Where people live will also impact on the type of schooling they have access to, and may restrict access to a more limited range of higher education institutions (e.g. those in the locale). The emphasis of interventions in both Australia and the UK however appears to be on promoting access to higher education, and less attention is given to the implications of cultural or social background for the higher education experience.

Parental education

Another approach to defining socio-economic status is to look at parental educational level, which is employed in the Netherlands, Norway and Sweden. For example, in Norway a sophisticated classification system is used, where the level of parental education is given a prominent role in

combination with employment type. Here, there are over a thousand occu-pational groups, divided according to type of occupation, level of education and degree of management responsibility. Similarly the Swedish system links parental education with occupation.

Although Canada uses employment as an indicator of socio-economic sta-tus, Canadian research has demonstrated the relationship between parental educational levels and participation in higher education (Statistics Canada 2002). For parents with a university degree there was an 88 percent rate of participation in post-secondary education by their children, with more than half of those entering post-secondary education going to university as opposed to college. College educated parents had a 68 percent rate of parti-cipation in post-secondary education by their off-spring, who were more likely to go to college than university. Parents with a high school diploma or less as their highest level of qualification had a 52 percent rate of participa-tion in post-secondary education by their children, with a much higher rate of participation in college rather than higher education. Similarly, longi-tudinal research in the US by the American Council on Education (ACE) found that a prospective student's likelihood of attending a four year college (as opposed to a two year community college programme) increases with the level of his or her parents' education (Choy 2002).

Data from Germany also indicate the significance of parental education (DSW/HIS 16th Social Survey, see Schnitzer 2003). The research compares the participation of students in different types of higher education (uni-versities and FH universities of applied sciences) in relation to the highest educational level of their fathers, in 2000. This finds that 49 percent of 19–24-year-olds have fathers with a lower secondary school leaving certificate (*Hauptschulabschluss*) as their highest qualification. Just 9 percent of these 49 percent attend a university and 7 percent of these 49 percent attend a university of applied sciences. These figures can be compared with the 30 percent of young people of the same age whose father's highest qualifica-tion is an intermediate secondary school leaving certificate (*mittlere Reife*). Of this 30 percent, 20 percent progressed to a university and 13 percent went to a university of applied social sciences. However, for young people whose fathers have a higher education entrance level qualification participation in higher education is significantly greater. Twenty percent of young people had a father with this level of qualification in 2000; of this 20 percent, 55 percent progressed to university and 20 percent to a university of applied sciences.

In the Netherlands detailed information is recorded about parental edu-cation, but very little about employment or income. In higher professional education (HBO) there are relatively more first generation entrants than studying at universities. In 2001 64 percent of first year HBO students had parents with no higher education experience. At universities 46 percent of students are first generation entrants, and this figure is lower in certain disciplines such as law and medicine/health (37 percent and 36 percent respectively). Differences between institutional types may be caused by a wide range of factors, including close links between HBOs and the

labour market. However, it is also worth noting that HBO institutions have a centralised admissions system based on a weighted draw for popular subjects, which helps to reduce the role of parental education and cultural capital in securing a higher education place.

Access and success of lower socio-economic groups/first generation entrants

Students from low socio-economic groups are constituted as some form of target in all ten countries but the way this manifests itself varies considerably and targeting may be explicit at the policy level, explicit at the level of decision making, implicit in regulations, or implicitly tied to financial incentives. This can be illustrated by comparing Australia, Ireland, US, Croatia and the UK.

In Australia and Ireland students from lower socio-economic groups form one of five key target groups and their needs are very explicitly addressed. Ireland is an interesting example of such targeting. Informed by legislation which requires universities to encourage greater access to the university by economically and socially disadvantaged sections of the community, (Universities Act 1997), Ireland has identified five target equity groups including people of low socio-economic status. It has adopted a strategic approach to changing this target into action by establishing an Action Group on Access to the Third Level whose report (Action Group on Access 2001) is currently informing all policy initiatives in the area, thus targeting works at all levels. In the USA although students from lower socio-economic groups are given more importance than any of the other groups, such tight regulation does not exist. Nevertheless the priority accorded to them clearly informs decisions made by institutions about their admissions and procedures. In Croatia there is no gathering of statistics at all in relation to this group, but each year the Ministry of Science and Technology reserves a certain quota for the priority enrolment of students who have passed the necessary examinations. These include diaspora, the children of those who died defending their country, disabled persons of the first degree and there is likely to be considerable overlap with low socio-economic status, so indirect targeting takes place. Although in Croatia academic ability seems to be the constant priority, those with low income are given financial support after qualifications are taken into account. In the UK, although no specific targets have been set with regards to the rate of participation by this group, the Higher Education Funding Council for England (HEFCE) has set benchmarks for each institution on the percentage intake from this target group and low participation neighbourhoods. No such financial incentives exist for ethnic minorities which seems to indicate that low socio economic status is being given priority. First generation entrants are not currently a target group in Australia, UK, US, Croatia, Germany or Ireland but they are targeted in Canada, Norway and Sweden. However, there are growing signs of

interest in using this categorization to identify and target under-represented groups.

Data issues

There is a wide range of data on these groups, from the very detailed to the non-existent. It is interesting to compare Sweden, UK, US, and Croatia in this respect as representing different patterns of data collection and consequently different levels of useful information gathered.

Sweden has a sophisticated process of collecting very detailed information, which might be seen as a model other nations should aspire to. Data concerning the target categories are almost exclusively found at Statistics Sweden. From here it is possible to obtain data on which socio-economic group students belong to, if they are first generation students and also their ethnicity. Data on socio-economic status for all students entering higher education are published every two years by Statistics Sweden, in cooperation with the National Agency for Higher Education in Sweden (see Higher Education. Social Background among University Entrants 2001/02 and First Time Postgraduate Students 2001, UF 20 SM 0202; see Forneng 2003).

The UK does not currently compare very favourably. Although statistics are collected by a multiplicity of national agencies they cannot tell us what we need to know about socio-economic status or first generation entry. The Higher Education Statistics Agency (HESA) does not publish data by socio-economic group, nor first generation entry and although data on parental occupation is collected on Universities and Colleges Admissions Service (UCAS) application forms, this is voluntary on the part of the student (with approximately one-third of applicants not supplying this information). This only covers those progressing via the UCAS system and not through other routes (including part-time applicants and direct entrants) which might be most predominantly taken by students from this target group. Nevertheless, it is a hopeful sign that it is envisaged data on first generation entry will be available for the higher education sector in the near future.

In the US rather than having a centralized system of collection of statistics, participation of these target groups is heavily 'documented' by the federal government. Since students are not required to report their family income, except for the purposes of applying for student financial assistance, such data is largely collected via by self-reported surveys and questionnaires. The Department of Education maintains many databases, including panel data from longitudinal studies which document the characteristics, conditions, and outcomes of low income students. The Department of Education has also amassed an extensive amount of data on this group from administrative records from federal, state and institutional sources. Verifiable data is maintained on family income, student financial aid awards, college curriculum grades, retention, persistence and graduation rates. In addition, the Department has data on time to degree attainment, enrollment status

(full-time, half-time and part-time), standardized test scores, high school curriculum and academic performance.

Croatia has no statistical data at all about low socio-economic groups or first generation entry. However, they do have certain assumptions about this group which seem fairly consistent with patterns observed in other nations, for example that such students will be more likely to attend polytechnics and are more likely to attend institutions in their own town.

Participation statistics

Access to tertiary education for students from lower socio-economic groups and first generation entrants is a problematic issue across the countries involved in the study. There is no country in which access for this group can be termed equal to those from higher socio-economic groups or those whose parents already have university qualifications. Another important factor to note is that socio-economic status seems to 'trump' other factors and be a higher determinant than being from a minority ethnic group, for example. However such divides are inherently artificial as low socio-economic status can often follow marginalized ethnicity and the incidence of disability increases with low economic status. For example, in the United States about 38 percent of black college undergraduates come from homes in the lowest income quartile, compared to 19 percent for white undergraduates. Also, only about 28 percent of black undergraduates come from a family where at least one parent had a Bachelor's degree, compared to about 44 percent for white undergraduates (NPSAS 2000). The central and mediating role of socio-economic status in all forms of disadvantage needs to be recognized. Dæhlen (2000, 2001) has found that in Norway it is social class origin which determines the difference in participation rates in higher education among immigrants from non-Western countries, making it lower than that of immigrants from Western countries and non-immigrants. Clark et al. note, 'that many low socio-economic status students are disadvantaged in other ways – sole parents, emotional trauma sufferers, long term unemployed, current or former offenders in custody' (Clark et al., in Ferrier and Heagney 2001: 52) and they conclude that low socio-economic status acts as a central determinant of disadvantage. Socio-economic status and the linked question of first generation entry need to be posed as the central and most pressing factor in addressing under-representation in tertiary education. However, as we have argued in Chapter 5, researchers who have looked at both indicators have found first generation entry to be even more determining of inequality in respect to Higher Education than socio-economic status.

In Australia it is estimated that people from low socio-economic status backgrounds make up 25 percent of the Australian population. The Commonwealth Government has set a participation target of 25 percent for this group. This is based on the premise that if the higher education student population is to reflect the diversity of the Australian population at large

then students from low socio-economic backgrounds should have a participation rate of 25 percent. However, despite large increases in overall participation in the higher education sector, this target group's participation has actually fallen from 14.7 percent in 1991 to 14.5 percent in 2002. It is estimated that on a per capita basis only five people from lower socio-economic backgrounds attend university for every ten people of medium or high socio-economic backgrounds (James 1999: 3). Large variations exist in access patterns between universities in the sector, although once enrolled these students' success and retention rates are close to those of the rest of the student body. Low socio-economic status students are under-represented in higher degree studies (research and coursework) and over-represented in sub-degree and enabling courses (Kemp 2000: 73). They are more likely to attend institutions which are newer and of lower status and are under-represented in the more prestigious professional disciplines (Postle et al. 1997).

In Canada in 1998, 39 percent of the 18–21-year-olds of the population from top quartile income families have attended university at one point or another in their lives, which represents a participation rate that is two times higher than those people from the same age group belonging to a lower quartile income (19 percent), (see Table 3.2).

For the low income family group, the participation rate rose from 13.7 percent to 18.3 percent (an increase of 3.5 percent), while the participation rate for the average income family group jumped from 14.5 percent to 25.3 percent (an increase of 10.8 percent). The data show that the gap between the lowest socio-economic status (SES) and the middle SES widened between 1986 and 1994, while the gap between the middle SES and the highest SES narrowed, see Table 3.3.

In terms of first generation entrants, high school graduates with university

Table 3.2   Post-secondary education participation and family after-tax income, 18–21-year-olds, 1998

Highest level of education participated	Lowest quartile (%)	Middle half (%)	Highest quartile (%)	Average (%)
All post-secondary (a)	56.1	62.2	69.7	62.7
University	18.8 (b)	27.5	38.7	28.4
College (c)	28.8	28.8	28.3	28.7

Source: Chenard and Bonin (2003)

Notes: (a) Includes universities, community colleges, institutes of applied arts and technology or *cégeps* as well as trade/vocational schools, but excludes business/commercial schools; (b) Estimates with relatively high sampling variability; (c) Includes community colleges, institutes of applied arts and technology or *cégeps*. Household income is defined as the annual after-tax income at the time the respondent was 16 years of age and living with his or her parents (expressed in terms of 1998 constant dollars). Values of quartiles: 'lowest quartile' is US$33,000 or less, 'middle half' is US$33,000–67,000 and 'highest quartile' is US$67,000 and more.

Table 3.3 University participation rate of 18–21-year-olds by socio-economic status (SES) of family

	Lowest SES (%)	Middle SES (%)	Highest SES (%)
1986	14.0	15.0	33.0
1994	18.0	25.0	40.0
1998	18.5 (a)	27.5 (a)	38.5 (a)

Sources: Chenard and Bonin (2003)

Notes: (a) Estimate. University participation rate is defined as a percentage of the 18–21-year-old population who have had at least some university education at the time of the interview.

Table 3.4 Proportion of students participating in post-secondary education, by parents' educational attainment

Parents' education	University (%)	College/cégep (%)	Trade–vocational (%)	Non-attendance (%)
Less than high school	30	34	* 9	27
High school diploma	33	32	7	28
Trade–vocational or college/*cégep*	43	34	* 6	16
University	67	18	–	13

Source: Chenard and Bonin (2003)

Notes: * High sampling variability. Highest level of either the mother's or father's education was used as a single measure of parents' education.

educated parents had higher odds of attending university (controlling for other factors). Nearly 70 percent of high school graduates with at least one university educated parent attended university, compared with 43 percent for those whose parents attained trade-vocational/college level (see Table 3.4). Only around 30 percent of graduates whose parents had high school or lower qualification participated in university education (Chenard and Bonin 2003).

Croatia does not keep any separate statistics on these target groups. However the fact that participation in higher education is generally extremely low in Croatia (see Table 3.5 below) might lead to the assumption that those who are already socially disadvantaged are not likely to make up many of this number. The majority of students study at the University of Zagreb, but it is believed that students with low socio-economic status sometimes choose to study at their local institution, possibly because this makes their living expenses lower.

In Germany social origin continues to be of decisive significance in the transition to higher education. Almost three-quarters of children with civil

Table 3.5   Population aged 15 or more according to the level of the finished school (in %)

1	NO EDUCATION	2.86
2	UNFINISHED PRIMARY EDUCATION	15.76
3	PRIMARY EDUCATION	21.75
4	SECONDARY EDUCATION	47.06
5	HIGHER EDUCATION	4.08
6	FACULTIES, ACADEMIES, M.A., M.S. and PhD	7.82
7	UNKNOWN	0.67

Source: Croatian Bureau of Statistics 2001

servants as fathers begin a course of academic study. Sixty percent of the children of independent professionals or freelancers take up university studies. In white collar households the rate is 37 percent, while in working-class (blue collar households) it is just 12 percent. In terms of first generation entrants, of those children whose father holds a higher education entrance qualification, three-quarters take up a course of higher education. By contrast, only one-third of those children whose father holds a 10th grade school leaving certificate (intermediate secondary – *mittlere Reife*) matriculate at a higher education institution, while only one in six of those children whose father only holds an 8th or 9th grade school leaving certificate (lower secondary – *Hauptschulabschluss*) does so.

In Ireland the contrast between those from higher and lower socio-economic status is particularly stark. Ireland is unusual in having data over a 20 year period on entry to third level education, and a clear longitudinal picture emerges (see Clancy 2001). Although the rate of admission to tertiary education has more than doubled over the past 20 years and proportionately participation by those from low socio-economic groups has increased the most, the distribution of access across socio-economic groups is very far from equal. Thus while the participation of those from the highest professional group (for example, those whose parents are university lecturers, doctors, dentists, accountants and lawyers) is virtually 100 percent, among unskilled and semi skilled manual workers participation is less than 25 percent.

In the Netherlands, first generation students, and by implication those from low socio-economic groups, seem to be accessing higher education at an accelerated rate, although they tend to be clustered more in the vocational domain than in that of the university. In higher professional education (HBO) two out of three students is a first generation student and at universities this is two out of five. However, there are indications that it is more difficult for them to access the most prestigious subjects such as law and medicine, here they have the lowest rate of participation, 37 percent and 36 percent respectively. The educational hierarchy also correlates with family income, as parents of university students on average earn 25 percent more than parents of HBO students.

In general, access to tertiary education in Norway has doubled over the last 20 years. However, only one-third of the students enrolled at universities and scientific colleges are first generation entrants, while two-thirds of those in state colleges have parents with tertiary education. There is a gender divide in that most men focus on the natural sciences while women are in the majority within health education and general subjects, but generally there are more females (61 percent) than males entering tertiary education. There is also evidence that the impact of social class origin varies to a large extent among educational fields and tends to be largest in 'soft' educational fields where performance is harder to measure and more affected by cultural factors (see Hansen 2001).

In Sweden data on the social background for entrants indicates that 26 percent have a working class background compared to 35 percent in the population. On the other hand, 25 percent of entrants are from the upper social classes compared to 18 percent in the population (data for new entrants in 2001/02). There are, however, institutional differences (see Table 3.6 below).

Table 3.6   Working class entrants in 2000/01

University	%	Representation
Uppsala	19	0.55
Lund	19	0.55
Göteborg	24	0.67
Stockholm	17	0.65
Umeå	29	0.75
Linköping	23	0.60
Karolinska institutet	23	0.77
Chalmers	22	0.59
Karlstad	33	0.79
Växjö	29	0.74
Örebro	30	0.76
Södertörn	33	0.81
Malmö	30	0.84
Total	**26**	**0.71**

Note: Number of working class entrants, percent of all entrants for a selection of universities. A representation figure below 1 means that working class students are under-represented.

In the UK in 2000, using the old SOC90 system, 40 percent of the population were classed as being skilled manual, semi-skilled or unskilled based on their current or most recent occupation (General Household survey 2000). Nationally a quarter of entrants to higher education aged under 21 come from this sector of the population. Most institutions take between 15 percent and 40 percent of young entrants from this group but just over 10 percent of higher education institutions are outside of this range (HEFCE (2003) performance indicators report 99–00, 00–01). UCAS data show that these

lower socio-economic groups made up 25.5 percent of the total entrants to 'new' (post-1992) universities in 2001 whereas they only made up 11.7 percent of the entrants to the 'old' universities. Table 3.7 shows the percentage of accepted applicants through UCAS for 2002 entry by the NS-SEC socio-economic groups.

Table 3.7 Home accepted applicants through UCAS by socio-economic group (2002 entry)

Socio-economic group	Accepted applicants to HE 2002	Total accepted applicants 2002 (%)
Higher managerial and professional occupations	66,556	18
Lower managerial and professional occupations	92,168	25
Intermediate occupations	44,753	12
Small employers and own account workers	21,009	6
Lower supervisory and technical occupations	13,238	4
Semi-routine occupations	36,010	10
Routine occupations	16,276	4
Unknown	78,105	21
Total	**368,115**	**100**

In the United States, low income students are disproportionately concentrated in two year colleges and correspondingly under-represented in the system's highest tiers. In 1998, 47 percent of lower income first-time, full-time freshmen who enrolled in college matriculated at public two year colleges, more than three times the rate of comparable upper income students (12.9 percent) and more than five times the rate of the richest students (8.1 percent) (McPherson and Schapiro 1999)[1]. Low-income students are acutely under-represented at traditional four year colleges. For AY 1999–2000, low income dependent students only comprised about 15 percent of the undergraduate student body at four year colleges and universities (NPSAS 2000).

The federal government's effort has failed to equalize college access across income and racial categories. Parental income still largely determines the likelihood of who earns a bachelor's degree. The gap between college enrollment rates of low-income students and their more affluent peers has widened in the last two decades. Also, the gap between the college enrollment rates of Whites and those of Blacks and Hispanics is larger now than it was thirty years ago. In addition, higher education institutions are demonstrably stratified by income and race.

(Upshaw 2003)

When low socio-economic status is linked to race the results are stark. Black and Hispanic students are more likely to be enrolled in community

colleges and terminal vocational programmes that are highly correlated with lower earnings and less social mobility (Mumper 1996). On average, the highest returns accrue to students attending and graduating from private four year institutions and the lowest returns are associated with students terminating with degrees from public two year colleges. Therefore, authentic equalized access is not attained if the traditionally non-college bound are disproportionately concentrated at the lowest tiers of post-secondary education (Karen 1991).

Retention and success

Although students from lower socio-economic groups and first generation entrants are under-represented in all ten countries participating in our international study, there are quite striking differences between the rates of retention and success for these student groups. It is interesting to compare the US, Australia, Sweden and the Netherlands. In the US low income students have significantly lower retention and degree attainment rates than their more affluent peers. For students at four year institutions, about 47 percent of dependent students in the lowest income quartile attain a Bachelor's degree within six years at their first institution and about 10 percent remain enrolled – equating to a 57 percent retention rate. In contrast, for this same timeframe, about 68 percent of students from the highest income quartile attain their Bachelor's degree and about 5 percent remain enrolled – translating into a 73 percent retention rate (BPS: 96/01; see Upshaw 2003). In Australia, however, retention rates for low socio-economic status are not significantly different from those of other students with an average rate of 75 percent retention across the board. Therefore, although access is a problem in both countries, rates of retention and success are very different. Clearly working class drop out is not the inevitability which is often suggested.

It is possible to isolate some of the factors which appear to be making a difference in Australia. Although the US has an overarching policy, the Higher Education Act (HEA) of 1965 which was hailed as a national promise to students from low income families that they would not face greater barriers to post-secondary education than their more affluent peers, it has not easily translated into action, largely it appears because the US system is driven by market forces and is multi-tiered. The US and Australian higher education systems provide some interesting comparisons. Foremost, the role of the central government is strikingly different. The Australian federal government has the principal responsibility for funding higher education, providing direct support through institutional enrollment grants. In contrast, the US government assumes a peripheral role, assisting higher education institutions through preferential treatment in the tax code and competitive research grant awards. In addition, the private sector role lies in stark contrast. Only two of Australia's 39 higher education institutions are privately

funded. In the US, private colleges comprise the majority of higher education institutions – 2484 versus 1698 (*Digest of Education Statistics* 2001; see Upshaw 2003). With respect to four year schools, private colleges outnumber public institutions almost 3 to 1 – 1828 versus 622 (*Digest of Education Statistics* 2001; see Upshaw 2003).

In Australia, having an integrated approach which creates correspondences at the national, meso- and micro-level is a key factor and the fact that this approach is now of long standing also plays a role. In *A Fair Chance for All* (DEET 1990) six groups, including those of low socio-economic status, were identified and designated as disadvantaged on the basis of their under-representation in the higher education student population, compared with their share of the population as a whole. The groups remain the primary focus of equity policies and programmes and are defined in precise operational terms. Indicators are constructed from institutional data collected annually by the Commonwealth Government. They measure the *access, participation, success* and *retention* of students in the target groups compared with other students and national equity targets. Individual institutions can use the indicators to monitor their progress towards the equity targets that they set themselves and to compare their results. This is a highly structured approach which seems to produce creative initiatives which have a rationale for their existence and ways of measuring success. However, the Australian example also illustrates how such an integrated approach can be threatened by other policy decisions which are inimical to it. For example, the decision to increasingly transfer the costs of study to students themselves is seen as undercutting progressive work with low socio-economic groups in Australia.

Sweden has looked closely at the issue of different rates of success among the target groups and has detailed centralized information on this issue. In a study based on new entrants in 1993/94 the National Agency of Higher Education in Sweden used data from Statistics Sweden to try to establish if there was any differences in results between students of Swedish or foreign background and between students from different social classes (see www.hsv.se). The study concluded that there are diffences in results depending on social and foreign background, but the differences are rather small: much smaller than the differences in number of students entering higher education from different backgrounds and much smaller than the differences in choices of study programmes, see Table 3.8.

Students from the upper classes have slightly better results irrespective of study programme than students from the working class, but the differences are rather small. The same is true for differences between students with Swedish or foreign background. This appears to suggest that some of the inequalities of access can be mitigated at an institutional level and is a hopeful indicator for the types of interventions we discuss in Chapter 7.

The Netherlands also provides a marked contrast. Their national report argues that neither the education nor the socio-economic status of parents seems to influence the study performances of students and that first

Table 3.8   Results for entrants in 1993/94 in Sweden

Education	Upper classes	Working classes	All entrants
Law	96	85	94
Civil engineering	93	89	90
Medicine	100	100	96
Nursing	91	83	89 *
Social work	91	89	91
Teaching, upper secondary school	92	92	93
Teaching, secondary school	93	90	91
Teaching, primary school	96	94	95
Liberal arts programmes	85	76	81
Shorter courses	70	53	61
Total	**79**	**71**	**74**

Notes: * Only students who have graduated. Percentage of students graduated or with at least 3 years of education.

generation students collect the same amount of credit as students with more highly educated parents, while students from lower income groups do as well as students from higher income groups. Various studies on drop out are quoted such as Prins (1997) and Van den Berg (2002, in Tupan–Wenno and Woolf 2003) which indicate that education of parents has no effect on study progress and drop out. In fact Van den Berg even concludes that 'SES-effects are sorted out in earlier phases of education [primary and secondary education] and that in university education the meritocratical process performs as it should be' (2002: 227, translation by Tupan–Wenno and Woolf 2003). However, meritocracy is not the only factor at play in the Dutch system and access to their tertiary education institutions is stratified according to education and income, with students from this target group over-represented in vocational areas, thus it is not the completely level playing field that this quote suggests. However, the emphasis on addressing factors of inequality in the early stages of the educational system is a crucial one and the flexibility of the HE system in the Netherlands is also beneficial to first generation entrants, as we shall discuss in Chapter 6.

The different patterns created by these different national systems seem to suggest that some of the disadvantages inherent in first generation entry can be redressed. Chapter 7 considers how national policy and institutional interventions have developed to support the access and success of students when the focus is on developing cultural and social capital, as opposed to compensating for low levels of economic capital.

Conclusions

Students from lower socio-economic groups are defined in a range of ways in the countries involved in our international study. These alternative approaches give differing weights to the financial and cultural capital that these families have access to and, in turn, the types of interventions that are implemented to support students from these groups to enter and succeed in higher education. These are themes which are discussed further in Chapter 5.

It appears that irrespective of how students from lower socio-economic groups are defined, they have lower rates of participation in higher education than students from higher socio-economic groups. Once in higher education however, rates of success are not necessarily lower for students from these groups. This suggests the need to further explore aspects of students' experience in higher education, how this relates to their access to social, cultural and financial capital, and how higher education systems and institutions can facilitate the success of students from non-traditional backgrounds.

Note

1 The study constructed six income categories: lower income (<US$20,000); lower middle (US$20,000–US$30,000); middle (US$30,000–US$60,000); upper middle (US$60,000–US$100,000); upper (US$100,000–US$200,000); and richest (>US$200,000).

4

Conceptualizing first generation entry

First generation entry and widening participation: an elusive concept

First generation entry remains quite an elusive concept and surprisingly little explored in the literature on widening participation. As discussed in Chapter 2, it is an international issue that needs defining as a 'problem' which requires a 'new zone of looking' (Novoa and Yariv-Mashal 2003: 437). In this chapter we will enter this new zone by moving beyond the literature on widening participation to draw on socio-cultural studies of the family. We will explain why parental education is worthy of investigation in its own right, as well as being strongly tied to class, and will present a workable definition of first generation entry to Higher Education. The chapter will explore first generation entry in terms of the changing nature of the family, the subjectification of the family and student in the dominant discourse of transition to university, the role of first generation entry in building social capital for the family and finally the family ambivalence provoked by first generation entry.

Although first generation entry seems the quintessential concern of widening participation, very few studies focus specifically on this issue. The recent comprehensive search of widening participation literature conducted for HEFCE (Gorard et al. 2006) revealed that only literature from the United States refers explicitly to first generation entrants to higher education. The term clearly has some currency in policy terms in the US: for example, the National Center for Education Statistics has reported on the access, persistence and attainment of first generation students and on the specific measures universities are using to support these students (NCES 2001). However, although they are identified as a significant category for government interest, there has been little attempt to engage with this issue on a theoretical level. London (1989) and Striplin (2000) point out the overlap between students who are the first generation in their family to enter university and students disadvantaged by poverty or race, but there is no coherent attempt

to theorize first generation entry. Canada has perhaps been at the forefront of statistical analysis linking parental education and class (see Chenard and Bonin 2003; Knighton 2002) and we shall return to their findings shortly. However, the British and other international literature, such as Reay et al. (2005) in the UK, Duru-Bellat (2000) in France, Lynch and Riordan (1998) in Ireland, Fair Chance for All (DEET 1990) in Australia, do not focus explicitly on first generation students but instead consider general issues of widening participation, patterns of choice, increasing access for students from variously disadvantaged backgrounds or increasing equality of participation via changes in university provision. Although various important studies consider families and cultural capital (see Reay et al. 2005) or include many first generation students (Archer et al. 2003; Leathwood and O'Connell 2003), first generation entry is not the specific focus of their research. We thus know a great deal about the experiences of such students, but not necessarily from the perspective of the influence of parental education.

Nevertheless, although first generation entry may not be spelled out in the literature and in policy making, there are certain shared assumptions that circulate. These are explicitly encapsulated by Knighton (2002) in a Canadian context:

> Parents educational attainment has remained a strong and persistent factor relating to post-secondary access. Parents with more education tend to share in their children's intellectual pursuits and pass down skills and beliefs that are conducive to achievement. They also get more involved in their children's education, have higher expectations for academic success and have greater familiarity with schools and teachers and with the post-secondary process and experience. the high value parents place on education can thus be transmitted when they actively provide their children with an environment that encourages educational attainment
>
> (Knighton 2002: 18)

It could be argued that any discussion of student disadvantage implicitly covers first generation entry and vice versa, and therefore there is no necessity to pinpoint the particular influence of parental education. However, we feel that this elides some important issues. Those who are first generation entrants are more likely to come from families which might be coded as working class by means of traditional indicators such as parental occupation or family income, but this is not inevitably the case. Those few researchers who have considered both first generation entry and socio-economic status have mostly found first generation entry to be more determining of inequality in respect to HE. In our international study an analysis of Statistics Canada data from 1993–98 discovered that

> of particular interest is the finding that young adults who had post-secondary education (college or university) and fell in the lowest income quartile were more likely to participate in post-secondary studies

themselves, compared with those whose parents were in higher income quartiles but without secondary education

(Chenard and Bonin 2003: 18)

In the USA, Horn and Nunez (2000) compared first generation students with their peers whose parents attended college. The study found that even after controlling for measures of academic achievement, family income, family structure and other related characteristics, first generation students are less likely than their peers to participate in academic programmes leading to college. In the US when considering only the most highly qualified students, those with college educated parents enrolled at four year institutions at a rate 16 percentage points higher than the potential first generation college students (ACE 2002). First generation entry does need to be placed within a matrix of class and ethnicity and as constituting a point of overlap of many factors. Indeed it is neither possible nor desirable to disentangle it from these strands. However, all these findings indicate that there is something distinctive and neglected about first generation entry and parental education.

Defining first generation entry

Once we start to look at this issue directly many questions and complexities emerge. There has never been an attempt to theorize what a first generation entrant might be, only a 'common sense' understanding. When first generation entry to university is discussed it is generally taken to mean that neither parent has had access to a university education and completed a degree. A student may not be 'first in the family' to go to university, if an older sibling has already entered, but they would still be of the first generation. We are most interested in the generational issue, rather than patterns among siblings, because, as we discuss in Chapter 6 it is the long-term developmental relationship within the family that has the most impact on educational progression and is most salient. The growing diversity of university provision makes it more difficult to measure this question. Does part-time day release to do a vocational qualification count as studying at university, does distance learning, does starting a course but not completing it? Is it only the kudos of a full degree that accords a parent university educated status? What happens if their degree is from another country and not recognized in this one? Is the real question one of distinction, so that with mass participation in university only those with postgraduate qualifications have sufficient cultural capital to make any difference? These are all questions that need working through. We have concluded that the parental opportunity to study at university is the fundamental factor in the definition, rather than type of course, duration or even completion. However, for a nuanced account, the nature of that opportunity is highly relevant. In socio-economic terms having a parent with a degree from Oxbridge, for example, confers more advantage than having a

parent with a two-year vocational qualification. Conversely in cultural and family terms the impact that such a vocational qualification might have in changing perspectives within the family could be more significant.

Since so few people went to university in the 1960s it could be argued that the majority of those who enter university today must necessarily be first generation entrants. However, although many parents may not have had the opportunity of university study immediately post-school, there has been a proliferation of part-time and work related educational opportunities and also large numbers of mature students. Those families with experience of university have consequently multiplied. First generation entrants, however, are those for whom the responsible older generation (not necessarily birth parents) have not had any opportunities to study at university at any stage in their lives. They are likely to be in occupations which do not permit university study, or they do not have the disposable income to pay for it. In Canada, where first generation entry has been targeted at a policy level, statistics indicate that in general parents' education is strongly linked to the family income: 'It is therefore impossible to completely disassociate first generation students from those belonging to a low socio-economic group' (Knighton 2002: 18). They have concluded that the most viable solution is to collect data on both categories and consider them together. We agree therefore that what it means to be first generation entrant is bound up in considerations of what it is to be working class, although a class focus does not completely encompass it. We try to proceed with this balance in mind and our definition of first generation entry aims to reflect changing family relationships, changes in patterns of participation in HE and the influence of socio-economic status.

Family theory and first generation entry

To understand first generation entry we need to trace social expectations about higher education and about the nature of the family within our society. First generation entry is a dynamic concept and multi-faceted: who is a first generation entrant and what that might mean is constantly subject to change. This understanding underlies our work in this book. We live in an age of diverse, fragmented and blended families which makes any categorizations linked to families very complex. Of course, families were never the ideal type beloved of policy makers, but there have been radical changes to what is now deemed (and permitted) to be a family. Families can no longer be assumed to consist of two biological parents and their children. Stepfamilies, single parent families, adopted families, families with gay parents, civil partnerships and families created with the help of assisted conception, all problematize the notion of family. Similarly families do not stay together in one place, different branches of the same family can exist across the country and internationally, and patterns of globalization, movements of refugees and greater social mobility all exacerbate this. Different ethnic

groups have different ideas of who might be included in their family. Some, such as homeless people, create their own families of those in similar situations and these families are fluid ones. Thus, theorizations of the family have changed emphasis from the structure of relationships to the quality of those relationships. They have expanded the analysis to include 'intimate relationships' which include associations between friends, sexual partners, family and kin (see Gillies 2003). All such diversity impacts up on the question of first generation entry. What happens, for example, if a step-parent has been to university but birth parents have not? What happens when families are dispersed over different countries and children are sent to live with university educated relatives? What happens when children are in care and are fostered or adopted by university educated parents? Can biology determine first generation entry, or is it more the collective resources of the older/responsible generation which are the determining factors? We would argue that it is the latter. When we come to look closely at qualitative data from research with first generation entrants in Chapter 6 it is evident that these looser family relationships are a reality and need to be taken into account.

There have been conflicting analyses of change within families. Some have seen the family as fragmenting and in decline with negative consequences both for individuals and society (see for example Murray 1994; Morgan 1995). Some have emphasized democratization and detraditionalization, arguing that greater individualization and a fragmenting of traditional structures has produced greater equality within the family, and new relationship structures, with an increased sense of choice and agency (Stacey 1996; Beck and Beck-Gernsheim 2002; Giddens 1999; Smart et al. 2001). Others, particularly feminists, have challenged this view. For example, Ribbens McCarthy et al. (2002) criticize Giddens's (1999) analysis of the democratic family, arguing that it may be more characteristic of the white middle class and thus pathologizes ethnic minority families. Jamieson (1998) suggests that there is little empirical evidence to support the thesis of democratization in the family, and Heelas et al. (1996) questions whether past beliefs have really been shed.

Mass participation in higher education could be seen to coincide with a supposed moment of democratization and individualization and indeed as a prime agent of this process. However, as exposed by Reay et al. (2005) democratization here, as elsewhere, is a gloss which hides little change or even regression. Their findings show that mass participation in the UK has not widened access to university and that proportionately fewer working class students go to university now than in the 1960s. Moreover, first generation entrants are predominantly gathered in certain types of university: post-1992 institutions with lower status. Families themselves often operate in inegalitarian and undemocratic ways to protect the interests of their members:

> The name of the school and university counts as a marker of attitude, soft skills and commitment . . . reputation is a classic public good and

social capital is likely to be deployed to protect it and to limit 'free-riders'. This can occur at all levels of the education system and suggests that parental engagement may operate to police boundaries to protect reputation and hence enhance the market value of the qualifications their children acquire

(Edwards et al. 2003: 20)

First generation entry cannot be seen neatly as the harbinger of either a democratic society or a democratic family.

The proponents of theories of the fluid family with a great capacity for social transformation, such as Giddens (1999), have been critiqued for lack-ing empirical evidence with which to substantiate their claims. It is useful to consider their arguments in the light of our empirical study of 67 ex-students who were the first in their family to go to university (Quinn et al. 2005; see also Chapter 6 of this book). This reveals that democratization and indi-vidualization are not the hallmarks of negotiations within these families and that these families seem more 'stuck' than fluid in terms of their structural positioning. It also suggests that Giddens may have in mind a middle class metropolitan family, which is very different from the provincial families in our study. On one level there are many accounts in which parents try (with varying degrees of success) to enforce their will upon their children:

Pete: I wanted to have a year off and then go to university. I was told not to do that.

Int.:   Who told you not to do that?

Pete: My parents. They said I wasn't having a year off. I was willing to get a job. They said, no, they said I wanted to just laze around. It is hard when you are living at home, because as much as you want to say no I want to do something else, you have to see them everyday and you are going to get moaned and nagged at. It is just easier to say I'll do it. So I did it.

(Pete, England)

In contrast to Beck and Beck-Gernsheim's (1998) 'individualisation thesis' where people become authors of their own life scripts and more free to pursue their own ends, our participants operated in the interests of the family and sometimes went against their own pleasures and desires to preserve the financial security and harmony of the family:

As much as I enjoyed the course and everything it was beginning to upset me as well as my mum . . . She was upset when I left, but I think for her I had to leave, because there is no way she could have kept up the financial payments, do you know what I mean, it was causing more fights me being at university than it was bringing any happiness

(Alan, Scotland)

This accords with the strand of thinking which understands family life as deeply moral and as a site of negotiated responsibilities (see, for example,

Holland et al. 2000; Ribbens et al. 2002). However, a form of discursive self-interest was also at play. Behaving in this way had another dimension, which was to preserve their status as 'family men' and with it the traditional rewards of working class masculinity, which in effect were fast disappearing with the decline of traditional industries (see Quinn et al. forthcoming). The indications were that despite economic and cultural change in these locations traditional gender divides and conventions had not significantly changed, and neither necessarily had the meanings ascribed to families and family relations.

It could be argued that our study, which is of those who were first generation to enter university but did not complete their course, demonstrates the pathology of families who are incapable of taking the opportunity to become fluid. However, this would disregard the wide range of constraints that produced withdrawal, such as finance and lack of familiarity with the system. It would also disregard the local specificity of family life where lack of economic opportunities, the power of nostalgia for the past and the limiting expectations of those such as careers advisers all seemed to produce young people and their families as 'stuck', even when their dispositions were potentially flexible (as discussed in Chapter 6):

> I think that people in the valleys they haven't got much confidence as a community you know . . . you get a sense of being knocked down and your family are the same, you know, not good enough, not good enough . . . well we're told not to make a fool of yourself in front of other people
>
> (Anna, Wales)

> I told the careers people I wanted to make films for a living but they told me I'd never be able to do that. They made me tick boxes on a computer. The number one jobs the computer came up with were stonemason, police officer and mechanic.
>
> (Stewart, Scotland)

So democratization, individuation, fluidity are not necessarily the most useful concepts with which to understand first generation entry and the family. Neither do concepts of the collapse of the family and the decay of society seem to be appropriate either, as these families demonstrated considerable cohesion and ways of holding themselves together. Rose (1996) challenges the linear narrative of detraditionalization and suggests a Foucauldian approach which focuses on the practices through which human beings are made subjects. If first generation entry is seen as a situated practice, what kind of families and subjects is it producing?

Transition to HE and the subjectification of first generation students and families

It is helpful here to focus on the dominant discourse of transition to university in order to understand the process of subjectification of first generation entrants and their families. On an international level there are common assumptions about transition to higher education and a particular positioning of first generation students within them. First, the first year is linked with notions of attrition: our study indicated that even in Sweden 30 percent of students withdraw in their first year. It is seen as a risky moment for which we must pave the way with specialist provision for those deemed at risk: such as providing summer schools for mature students in Ireland and specialist induction for ethnic minorities in Norway. It is a time of probation, and this is formalized in some systems: in Norway over 25s are admitted without qualifications but only on probation until they pass their first year. The first year is a time of integration, with study skills mentoring and tracking increasingly embedded in curriculum and validation, following the lead of Australian universities such as Monash. It is also considered to be a time of stress with psychological consultations routinely offered to mature students in Croatia, for example. Late or interrupted transitions to the first year are seen as problematic in the United States with going to university straight from school being associated with persistence.

In the UK, HE policy depicts transition to higher education as the fulfilment of a goal that large numbers of young people should cherish. It is considered desirable for the good of society that 50 percent of those under 30 should experience higher education by 2010. Transition to HE is represented as a change in status, as a culmination of aspirations to be a better person with better opportunities and ultimately the route to better citizenship: 'HE also brings social benefits . . . there is strong evidence that graduates are more likely to be engaged citizens' (DfES 2003a).

The emphasis has been on the moment of access, the pivotal moment of change, and far less attention has been paid in policy, practice or even research, to what happens once students reach university. This transition has been dominantly conceptualized as a youthful one, as part of an unproblematic and seamless path to incorporation in successful life. Anything that appears to threaten this transition, such as early withdrawal, must be regulated and suppressed. Non-retention is seen as 'setting students up to fail' and as 'unacceptable' (DfES 2003b). HEFCE, the English Higher Education Funding Council, has been tasked with 'bearing down' on those institutions that allow it to happen (DfES 2003b).

If our findings on first generation entry from the Joseph Rowntree Foundation study are considered in relation to transition, they show that the students involved actually experience both less and more of a transition than is generally posited. For many of these young people nothing dramatically changed, in fact going to university may have secured stasis for them more

than other choices such as employment would have done: they carried on living at home with their family; instead of leaving the house for school or college they left to go to university; they often went along with the same crowd of friends they had had in school; and they generally continued with the same part time jobs. The university, rather than ushering in a new life, facilitated a continuation of the old one. As one research participant commented: 'Go to school come home, go to university come home, nothing different'. In other respects the transition was more dramatic than policy makers might imply. They did not enter the university on equal terms, they were not familiar with its academic practices, its norms or its values and could not gain guidance from their parents. They did not generally have the assurance to claim the support and servicing that middle class students increasingly expect as a right.

In policy terms, leaving early means that their move into university was a failure. The students themselves did not interpret it this way. For policy makers, leaving is seen as the end of the road, a calamitous loss and waste. For the young people it was part of a process of change and reassessment, of learning what they did not want, as well as what they did as we shall discuss further in Chapter 6. All but one wanted to return to education, and most felt they had gained positive experience from their time at university. They wanted opportunities to go part-time, transfer courses, leave and return without penalty. In this sense, they needed a flexible system to accommodate a fluid learning self. This flexibility did not exist. In structural terms: institution and students are financially penalized for non-completion, change to part-time or other courses was not encouraged and mobility was seen as an aberration – to be feared rather than encouraged. In cultural terms withdrawal was understood as a predictable symptom of working class propensity to failure and the students were mostly regarded and treated in these terms by those such as employment agencies and employers.

As we have suggested, the prevalent notion of transition as a fixed turning point which takes place at a pre-ordained time and in a certain place does not accord well with our research findings on first generation entry. Entering university did not mean making a transition into a qualitatively different life and the point at which the student is ready for HE may occur long in the future, after they have withdrawn and reformulated their priorities. However, other notions which link transition to identity and as a process of 'becoming somebody' (see Ecclestone et al. 2005: 1) are equally problematic, because they still suggest a unified humanist subject capable of being transformed by education. Authenticity is still the hallmark of this discussion, whereas it is more useful to understand the students as engaged in multiple performances. For example, the young men in our study were involved in performances of whiteness and masculinity which drew on cultural narratives such as nostalgia for the security and solidarity of 'lost' white jobs such as pottery and mining (see Quinn et al. forthcoming for a full discussion). Transition as a question of having a 'story to tell', as discussed in Ecclestone et al. (2005: 1) implies that there is an individual, meaningful

narrative generated from the student themselves. In fact students employ many interlocking narratives drawn from culture, for example the story of the young working class man as rebel and as family man, in order to negotiate movements into and out of university.

Ecclestone et al. suggest that 'some transitions are never complete but have to be reworked continually' (2005: 2). While we would agree that issues of class, race and gender make it more difficult for some people to authoritatively claim the final change in personal status that university education is supposed to confer, the idea that the self is constantly reworked is actually pertinent to everyone. It is not only where the person is in some sense displaced from the 'norm' that this process will be perpetual. We would argue that we are all always lost in transition, not just in the sense of moving from one task or context to another, but as a condition of our subjectivity:

> . . . the subject is not an 'entity' or thing, or a relation between mind (interior) and body (exterior). Instead it must be understood as a series of flows, energies, movements and capacities, a series of fragments or segments capable of being linked together in ways other than those that congeal it into an identity.
>
> (Grosz 1993: 197–8)

The fact that transition is normal rather than strange might suggest that we should all be able to cope well with it. If structures were flexible then this might be possible. One could argue that the students in our study wanted to normalize multiple transitions in and out of education in line with their postmodern sensibility. As we shall discuss in Chapter 6, it is partly their parents who foster this flexible attitude to education: that it is not all or nothing but simply another aspect of life. However, systems and policies ensure that transitions are moments of crisis which must be traversed well or not at all, and a linear pathway suggests there is no going back and no opportunity to take an interesting byway.

Transition implies that one moves from one state to another, one has gone through a change and become different *because of* the external event. This is too static a viewpoint. We constantly change, we transform, we move backwards and forwards, we do not coalesce either before or after even the most momentous life crisis. Policy makers (and certain kinds of educators) clearly enjoy the notion of transition because they can form a pathway and lead others along it to goals (and learning outcomes) that are predefined, neat and orderly. For first generation entrants the process of transition is located as a shedding of the old and the inadequate self in favour of one that is new and improved. Thus the first generation entrant is understood as one who must allow themselves to be changed. In practice there are resistances to this: the first generation entrant is by no means a blank slate or empty vessel. This leads us to a consideration of social capital and its role in first generation entry.

Family, social capital and first generation entry

We believe that debates on social capital are apposite to the discussion on first generation entry and that we can build on our previous work in this area (see Thomas 2003; Quinn 2005). Bourdieu in particular has proved fertile ground for educationalists (see Reay et al. 2005). He sees social capital as 'the aggregate of the actual or potential resources which are linked to the possession of a durable network of more or less institutionalised relationships of mutual acquaintance and recognition' (Bourdieu [1986] 1997: 47–51). Membership of a group confers social capital but has to be permanently worked at. The nature of the social capital is shaped by the material cultural and symbolic status of the family. He has been used very effectively, and some would say ubiquitously, to demonstrate how education functions as cultural capital and as a marker of distinction which is fiercely fought over by families.

Education has received some attention in other sociological discussions on families and social capital, but we would argue not nearly enough. So, for example, Coleman (1990) argues that the ability of parents to devote interest and support to their children increases the likelihood of producing human capital in the form of educational achievement. It is in the long-term interest of families to invest in their children and in turn the sustainable family will produce a stable and productive society. This view of families and education clearly underlies New Labour initiatives in the UK from Sure Start at pre-school level, onwards, to 50 percent widening participation targets for higher education. Although there have been major family studies conducted in the UK which specifically address the family in transition, in particular the ESRC Families and Social Capital research group, none of them really address how families produce first generation entry or how first generation entry changes the family. Some consideration has been given to education, mainly at the schooling level, but the conclusion is that some areas of higher education require much more study: 'The expansion of avenues of higher education and the role of teachers as mentors together with parental and student networks in routes to degrees, in an ever more differentiated higher education system. Social capital research has yet to address these areas and answer these sorts of questions.' (Edwards et al. 2003: 22).

Most significantly of all, what we might call the reciprocal relationships between children and parents tend to be neglected within discussions of families and social capital. As Edwards argues 'absent are conceptions of children as active participants in shaping the nature of family life and caring relationships, and in generating social capital for themselves, parents siblings and other family members' (2004: 8). We would argue that first generation entry fits this reciprocal dynamic conception of family relations: operating at multi-levels upon the family and its development. Thus it requires a fresh approach to social capital. So first generation entrants are not simply the recipients or the markers of a family's social capital but active producers and catalysts in (potentially) changing the nature of family life

and the patterns of family behaviour and the world in which the family lives. We are conceptualizing first generation entrants as pivotal and even totemic figures, not only for the family but for the culture, with a structural and a discursive function as well as a relational one. The first generation entrant is required to do a great deal of work: perfect themselves as educated and employable; reassure the family that they have 'invested wisely'; open up the aspirations and horizons of the family and its community; represent a triumph of social egalitarianism; and prove that 'everyone can make it'. In Foucauldian terms they are in the process of being produced as certain kinds of subjects *for* society, not just in society. They are locked in a particular operation of power/knowledge under a regime of truth that university education is good, necessary and even the only option.

Skeggs's (2005) ideas on class, self and exchange value are useful here: we must interrogate what this educational opportunity of being the first generation in a family to enter university represents within culture, how it is branded. First generation entry is culturally specific and so is the form of social capital produced. In the UK, the degree they are studying for on one level is highly desirable, even obligatory, on the other hand it is likely to be of an 'inferior' brand: not an elite subject and not in an elite institution. They are compelled to buy something that may ultimately be of little value, but they can't afford to be without it. This produces a high level of ambiguity. In Croatia, on the other hand, where a very small number of people enter HE, first generation entry will have much more elite connotations and consequences, but it is not necessarily a prerequisite for citizenship (Vidaceck-Hains 2003).

First generation entrants, however, are not simply passive dupes, they are producing forms of power for themselves and the family, so the questions might be, assuming there is some form of social capital generated: What kind? Who is it for? and, How is it used? Taking the UK as the example, the social capital may not lie in the degree itself, but within the prevailing discourse of aspiration and mobility, Students have demonstrated that they can be winners in this discourse and not losers. So the first generation entrant gains knowledge and qualifications, but most importantly is brought into the fold. They are insiders not outsiders of the educational and social project and so can begin to be social capitalists. They bring their family into the fold with them and then they can all begin to barter and play. How this then works out in practice is highly complex and differentiated by age, ethnicity, locality and so on, but this discursive level is the key to understanding the process.

There are many discussions about the different definitions of social capital (Field and Schuller 1997; McClenagahan 2000). Dasgupta (2002) notes: 'There is no single object called social capital, there is a multitude of bits that together can be called social capital. Each bit reflects a set of interpersonal connections' (2002: 7). Debates have identified at least four different types of social capital: bonding, bridging, linking and imagined social capital. It is

worth considering how first generation entry might fit within this typology. Coleman's (1990) view of 'bonding' social capital is that it is the glue that ties families together and produces shared values within them and among families like them. Bridging capital (Puttnam 2000) refers to the trust and connection forged between different sorts of people in different walks of life, fostered by such activities as volunteering, which is outward looking and particularly good for society. Linking social capital (Woolcock 1998) is the ability to access resources from formal institutions, including for example Higher Education. Imagined social capital (Quinn 2005) refers to the bene-fit produced by imagined and symbolic networks which people create to re-imagine themselves and their lives. All these concepts tend to produce an idealized type against which the fallible person and their family must inevit-ably be found lacking. Bonding and bridging capital in particular have tended to be adopted by social policy, evoked in a prescriptive way and as injunctions to act rather than as an observation of processes. The danger of the discussions as they have progressed so far is that families with diverse unbonded values must inevitably be non-functioning, that certain types of social networks, often pursued by men are valorized and that imagined social capital is connoted as belonging more to women. As well as using social capital to understand first generation entry, first generation entry may help to expand thIs debate on social capital.

First generation entry cannot necessarily be assumed to produce bonding social capital. As we shall discuss, it can create fractures rather than glue. There is some research in the field of family studies on the effects of a family member being the first to pursue a university education: including the effects on the marital relationship (Cooney et al. 1982); on wider kinship ties (McAdoo 1978); and on intergenerational bonds (Crosnoe and Elder 2002). In all of these studies first generation entry produced tensions and difficul-ties which were not necessarily easy to resolve, and problematized rather than cemented ideas and values. The problem is that policy assumes that education will inevitably be a shared value and that opportunities to access it will further family and social cohesion: 'The social gap in entry to HE remains unacceptably wide . . . It means a waste of potential for individuals and the country as a whole' (DfES 2003b). This is why the discourse on 'drop out' is so pejorative: those who withdraw early threaten stability on many levels. However, these studies also seem to suggest that given time, first gen-eration entry can help to foster new sets of values within the family, more critical perhaps, but very useful to the continuing renewal of the family. If bonding can be seen to include and embrace mutual questioning then first generation entry might contribute to these bonds. Bonding has been seen as sharing and believing the same things, but it is possible that families could share the attitude that they are unsure, doubting and critical and that first generation entry could foster this.

Turning to bridging social capital, first generation entry is predominantly seen as an opening out into the world and this is couched in the language both of opportunity and of citizenship (see the White Paper, *The Future of*

Higher Education, DfES 2003a). The problem here is that building bridges depends not only on the will to do it, but on being structurally able to do it. Whose time was given at home so bowling teams could meet and play together, to use Puttnam's classic example of desirable bridges? Who will be accepted on to the team? So first generation entry depends upon a network of support from family and friends and it also depends on acceptance by others. How easy is it for black and minority ethnic groups to build bridges in those universities where they are tiny minorities, however great their desire for bridging social capital? (Connor et al. 2004). The evidence is extensive that bridges are not easy for first generation entrants (Archer et al. 2003; Leathwood and O'Connell 2003) and in our study there were often examples of being stranded and isolated on what seemed like a lonely island with no way off: 'I just felt so alone and as if there was no-one out there who could possibly help me'. Nevertheless, there are indications that university study is an important means by which strangers can meet and make connections (Thomas 2002); one of the vital resources for making strange and new in our culture (Quinn 2005). 'I used to be the sort of person who never said anything but being at university I got the chance to meet so many different people that I would never have had a chance to before and it really helped build my confidence'. Thus bridging social capital gaps can be a consequence of first generation entry, not simply for the student but for their family networks.

It is clear that opportunities to create linking social capital via access to formal institutions is very much classed and raced. Generally the family of the first generation student does not know how such institutions work and is not confident in negotiating with them:

Int.:   Who was influential in helping you to reach your decision [to leave]?

Student: I just spoke with my parents. My friends at university were disappointed and wanted me to stay on. My project group tried to get me to stay. My parents didn't influence me either way. They said it was up to me. But I don't think they had the experience in it.

However, being totally deprived of links to universities can decrease social capital, particularly when university degrees are a prerequisite even for jobs that appear unskilled. An employer from a major call centre company who took part in the English research jury day (see Chapter 6) described the large pool of graduates from whom he was able to pick his labour force. He was aware that for families this job destination often seemed demeaning and not what they had hoped for: 'families say don't go to a call centre its like a chicken farm or something'. Nevertheless, the reality was that without a degree even this job might be closed, so scarce are the opportunities in this locality: 'there are jobs, yes, but good jobs very few' (student).

The final category, imagined social capital, does not ignore inequality but rather can be produced by shared 'outsider knowledge' of exclusion and

hard times, as well as imagined links with mythological communities (Quinn 2005). Potentially, first generation entrants are in a better position than others to create this form of capital because, not in spite, of the marginal positions their families often occupy in society. This is important as we must guard against a deficit model of first generation entry which posits them as lacking. Nevertheless, Bourdieu reminds us that it is only capital which is legitimated that counts. More specifically, Preece (1999) illustrates that the social capital owned by some sectors of society is simply not valued by higher education because '. . . the nature of what counts as valuable social networks is still culturally defined' (Preece 1999: 13). The most important issue for first generation entrants and for their universities is how to legitimate and employ the knowledge they bring with them (Thomas 2003). The evidence suggests that this is not a common occurrence. For example Quinn (2003) in her study of the mass participation of women and the mainstream curriculum found that working class women were often the most analytical and intellectually advanced of students, able to critique the curriculum because their positioning revealed to them its gaps and lapses. However, these insights were rarely acknowledged or deployed by their lecturers.

First generation entry can therefore be instrumental in developing all these different types of social capital for the family: bonding, bridging, linking and imagined. In some respects these families can be seen as those most in need of social capital and therefore the outcome seems positive in terms of mobility. However, the consequence of gaining such capital may be to move the family in directions that seem problematic, thus causing ambivalence, as we shall discuss.

The ambivalence of first generation entry

In practice, first generation entry is contested, paradoxical and ambivalent. In Foucauldian terms, it involves students working on themselves and becoming 'disciplined bodies' who will do what is expected of them and want to do it, but it will also evoke counter-memories and counter-narratives which make this process far from straightforward. Theoretical approaches to the family include the introduction of the concept of sociological ambivalence (Connidis and McMullin 2002) which may be a useful tool in our investigation. Here ambivalence is defined as 'simultaneously holding opposing feelings or emotions that are due in part to countervailing expectations about how individuals should act. Thus ambivalence reflects the contradictions and paradoxes of social experience' (Connidis and McMullin 2002: 1). These are socially structured contradictions made manifest in interaction. Within the family, these ambivalences are enacted and negotiated. This view of the family recognises structural inequalities perpetuated by the family: 'Current familial arrangements benefit some groups more than others and "the family" is one institution through which current inequalities

are enforced', (Connidis and McMullin 2002: 566). However, the family may also be trying to manoeuvre itself out of an unequal position, and first generation entry might be conceived of as a key lever to do that. Nevertheless, this is not the straightforward process that the rhetoric of aspiration implies and it is not something that happens suddenly. The meaning of education for the student and the family is not always apparent. For example, many of our participants in the drop out study had to leave university before they could understand its value:

> Int.:   Would you recommend going to university to other people?
> Student: I would recommend it . . . People need to know what they
>   want to do and what they want to get out of it. Not just
>   jump in

Connidis and McMullin (2002) focus on difficult situations with which a family must contend, such as care of an elderly relative, arguing that they make ambivalence particularly visible. Although first generation entry is less clearly problematic, and may indeed be a successful culmination of a family dream, it does represent a moment of disrupted order within the family and so is susceptible to ambivalence. Connidis and McMullin attempt to bring together critical and interactionist aproaches in their article. We would wish to add a post-structural perspective, recognizing that much of the ambivalence occurs at the discursive level, where different cultural narratives about what it is to be educated and working class collide. We might identify a number of such ambivalences. Parents want children to go to university but fear that this may result in abandoning the family and its norms and values. Children may not want to go to university but feel they must to fulfil their parents' ambitions, and compensate for past inequalities: 'My mum wanted her son to be a university student' (male participant JRF research). It is well documented that when the first in the family to enter is the wife and mother, the non-participants feel the threat of the loss of the old order and can manifest this in resentment and sabotage (see, for example, Edwards 1993). This can even result in the woman having to act as if they are not really attending, nullifying and masking their new position as a student. Sometimes both parents and children may do everything possible to facilitate university entry but also undermine the possibility of success by manifesting ambivalence. Participants in our JRF study repeatedly said that their parents only wanted them to be 'happy', did not 'really mind' if they stayed in university or not, while at the same time stressing the importance that their parents had accorded university education. This scenario is driven not by individual or family pathology, but by conflicting cultural narratives about being a loyal family member and being an educated person, about being true to class and family history, but also being free to take the family further. It is enacted within a highly problematic socio-economic framework, where traditional industries have been replaced by a rhetoric of educational access, but it is by no means clear that this will provide any adequate compensation or assured reward:

> I live on a council estate . . . people from that kind of place think that education isn't important and you're getting that drummed into you all the time. That you don't need to get an education, get a job, go into an industry but industry is very low now in this area. The effect of 'drop out' on the community is morale as well . . . they hear you saying 'oh I couldn't manage it at university' and they think 'oh maybe I shouldn't go either'
>
> (participant facilitator/student who had dropped out)

Theoretical positions on families and memory are also useful in this discussion. Memory may act in ambivalent ways as a familial resource. For middle class families university memories act as a store from which recent entrants can benefit. Thus the cultural and social capital of going to university: prestige, access to certain jobs, useful and influential networks are cached in the family memory vaults. However, for first generation entrants, memory passed on of education deprivation and inequality can also be used as a spur. For example, women may want to take hold of what was withheld from their mothers and grandmothers and so access a university education (see Quinn 2004b).Thus first generation entry can be a manifestation of deep ties and links within the family and a psychosocial phenomenon that takes us far from the mechanical calculations of targets and target groups.

Conclusion

Researchers in family life, and in particular in intergenerational ties, have noted, 'the limited development of theoretical concepts and perspectives', and the need for:

> multilevel analysis that connects interactions within families to social structure and culture, the importance of viewing conflict as a central feature of social life, the need to focus on relationships and families rather than on individuals exclusively and the necessity to consider diversity in family life.
>
> (Connidis and McMullin 2002: 1)

We concur, having found theoretical conceptions of first generation entry virtually non-existent and recognizing that this topic needs approaching from a range of interconnected perspectives. Our understanding is informed by a theoretical and empirical investigation of first generation entry. We have drawn on theories about transition, families, social capital, sociological ambivalence and cultural memory, on our international study of widening participation and our UK wide study of first generation entrants.

Taking into account the changing nature of families, the changing patterns of participation in HE and the influence of socio-economic status, we have defined first generation entrants as those for whom the responsible older generation (not necessarily birth parents) have not had any opportunity at

any time in their lives to experience university education. We conclude that it is virtually impossible to disentangle first generation entry from social class, and neither is it desirable to do so. Lack of opportunities to study at university mostly occur because of inequalities in school level provision, because people are not in jobs which include access to university-based training and do not have the money to fund it themselves. However, our international research indicates that a parent's education, largely shaped by class, is the most determining factor in their children's access to higher education, and it is this particular relationship which is least explored and least understood, despite the many existing studies of working class students.

Current theories of the family as dangerously fragmenting or positively individualistic and democratic have tended to lack an empirical basis. We have been able to use our empirical study of first generation students to question these positions and to support those which emphasize the reciprocal relationships within families with their ethical and moral impulses, and which lead family members to act for the good of the whole family rather than themselves. Trying to understand first generation entry as a process of subjectification for student and family we have deconstructed the dominant discourse of transition to argue that the first generation student is positioned as one who must change themselves, and who must prove that the family has now made it into the arena of responsible and respectable citizenship signified by university education. However, we have argued that the student already has social capital and is not an empty vessel, although this social capital may well not be recognized or validated by the university. First generation entry can be understood as a means of building further stocks of bonding, bridging, linking and imagined social capital for the family, even though this can be a messy and difficult process. Nevertheless the disruption to the family signified by first generation entry, as provoking clashes between the aforementioned loyalty to the family and the dominant discourse that the family must move and change, produces ambivalence, and this ambivalence is perhaps the key motif of first generation entry.

Ultimately first generation entry is a contradictory and indeed conflicted position which represents a crossroads for the family from one mode of being outside the university into one where the family is both inside and outside, drawing on memory to negotiate and make sense of this situation. This position can be seen as both inhibited and potentially liberated. The first generation students in our UK study were structurally and culturally restricted by lack of knowledge about universities and how they worked, because their families had not had the opportunity to build up this store of experience. However, they were also potentially more flexible in aspiring to move in and out of learning rather than feeling irrevocably committed to staying for three years without a break. It is possible to argue that not being shaped by the norms of university study liberates these students into a more flexible lifelong learning mode. They are structurally disadvantaged but at the same time potentially intellectually well positioned. Nevertheless, because of concomitant factors related to lack of employment opportunities,

restrictive cultural norms, the limited expectations others have of them and structural rigidity of the HE system they are fixed in a limited position which does not encourage or facilitate this flexibility. An international perspective reveals that this is very much shaped by nationality. A student in the Netherlands, for example, would not have to contend with this inflexibility within the HE system, whatever their family background. So the condition of first generation entry is a product of national educational norms as well as socio-cultural positioning.

In this theoretical discussion we have explored ways in which first generation entry can be understood and have demonstrated that it is a rich and complex subject worthy of close investigation. These understandings inform our ongoing discussions, which will proceed in Chapter 5 to focus on the international evidence concerning the influence of parental education on the access and participation of first generation entrants in university.

5

The potential impact of parental education on access and success in higher education

Introduction

Having discussed how first generation entry is linked to the generation of various forms of social capital within the family in Chapter 4, the overall purpose of this chapter is to proceed to exploring how parental education may impact on access to higher education and students' experiences within HE. Our focus will shift to issues of economic and cultural capital. The discussion about the participation and success of students from lower socio-economic groups in Chapter 3 identified four key ways in which this concept is operationalized: income, occupation, geography and parental education. For us this raises a key question about the relative significance of financial and cultural factors in relation to progression into and through higher education. This is examined by considering the evidence from the literature about the financial barriers to widening participation and then considering the impact of cultural barriers. The potential impact of parental education is analysed by examining literature and research about the contribution of parental education on early development and achievement and the relationship between parents, schooling and progression to higher education, the transition into HE and experiences within HE. The chapter concludes by identifying the potential impact of parental education on access to and experiences in higher education for first generation entrants. This informs our analysis of first generation entrants experiences in higher education in Chapter 6.

Economic and cultural capital

The discussion of socio-economic status in Chapter 3 indicates how national definitions of 'lower socio-economic groups' are related to four types of categorization: income, employment, geography and education. These labels apply differential weights to the significance of family stocks of, or access to,

economic and cultural capital, which in turn shape and influence the strategic and practical approaches to widening participation that are adopted.

Many definitions of lower socio-economic groups incorporate a lack of access to financial resources, and this is seen to be of growing importance as the cost of higher education is increasingly being shifted from the tax payer to the student (and their family). One of the consequences of focusing on a lack of economic capital is, for example, to concentrate on the provision of financial aid and bursaries as a primary way of widening access and supporting students to complete their course.

Parental education provides access to cultural capital, which is the knowledge, language, values, experiences and ways of doing things that belong to the dominant social group. Cultural capital is tacit, and largely transmitted through the family (Reay 1998), although it is created, reinforced and replicated by the education system (Bourdieu and Passeron 1977). Bourdieu's analysis of French higher education concluded that working class students were less successful, not because they were of inferior intelligence or not gifted, but because the curriculum was, 'biased in favour of those things with which middle-class students were already ex-curricularly familiar' (Robbins 1963: 153). In other words, educational institutions favour knowledge and experiences of dominant social groups (for example, white, middle class men) to the detriment of other groups. In relation to widening participation, a focus on cultural capital may seek to influence attitudes towards higher education, developing an understanding of higher education norms and practices and providing young people and their parents with 'insider knowledge' about HE that those whose parents have participated in HE have ready access to. Ultimately it brings into question the nature of the curriculum itself and the need to reassess what counts as knowledge; but this curricular debate seems to be a long time coming (see Quinn 2006).

Efforts to widen participation in higher education may focus on economic or cultural capital approaches, or a combination of these, as presented above. This raises a key question about the relationship between economic and cultural capital, and what sort of policies and interventions should be developed to maximize the access and success of first generation entrants in higher education. This question is now considered by reviewing the evidence about financial and cultural barriers to access and success in higher education.

Financial barriers to access and success

Student financial issues have frequently been identified as a barrier to access and success in higher education. Qualitative research in the UK (Thomas and Jones 2003) identified four ways in which finance can create barriers to access and success:

1. Actual lack of money and concern about debt.
2. Comparative lack of money in relation to friends not in HE, or previous periods of employment, and, for mature students in particular, guilt about not contributing to the family income.
3. The need to supplement income through 'part-time' employment.
4. Difficulties and hostility regarding the transition from welfare benefits to being a student.

(Thomas and Jones 2003: 146)

In the UK the shifts towards students and their families, rather than tax-payers, paying for higher education are expected to have a negative impact on the participation of students from lower socio-economic groups, particularly low-income families (Education and Employment Committee 2001; Dearden et al. 2004a). This is, at least in part, because the expected levels of debt of students from working class backgrounds are 46 percent higher than the average £10,000 debt (UNITE 2005; see also Metcalf 2005). However, a study of participation rates between 1994 and 2000 (HEFCE 2005) found no evidence that the introduction of tuition fees and the replacement of grants with loans had significantly affected entrant behaviour. In Australia, where student fees were introduced in 1989, the proportion of young people from the lowest socio-economic backgrounds attending HE has remained largely unchanged, while the overall participation rate has increased (Chapman and Ryan 2002).This suggests that an income contingent loan system may be fairly neutral in its impact upon widening participation.

Research with prospective students in the UK (Callender 2003) paints a rather different picture, however. The study of nearly 2000 UK school and further education college leavers working for HE entry qualifications concludes that, other things being equal, debt tolerant prospective students were one and a quarter times more likely to enter HE than debt averse students. Those who were most debt averse were those from the low income social classes, lone parents, Muslims (especially those of Pakistani origin), and black and minority ethnic groups. In McGrath and Millen's study (2004) six out of 21 respondents cited financial reasons for withdrawing once they had received an offer of a place, mostly before receiving their A-level results. Among those still undecided about HE entry, perceived financial barriers were a major cause of their indecision and once again those from lower income social classes were more likely to mention concern about their ability to afford HE (Callender 2003). Australian research with prospective students (James 2002) also suggests that fear of debt discourages students from lower socio-economic groups. But in Connor's (2001) survey in the UK, many potential students seemed resigned to ending up in some debt: it was a consequence of being a student, although there was some evidence that financial concerns were more of an issue for students from poorer homes.

It is not clear from these research studies whether finance is a barrier *per se*, or whether it is a barrier because higher education is not sufficiently valued by some groups. The former is more likely to effect low income students,

while the latter may have greater impact in low income families with no history of higher education.

The Universities UK study (Callender 2003) concluded that the level of funds available to HE students through the student support system were, at the time of the survey, a barrier to widening participation. Lack of certainty about access to discretionary funding was found to act as a deterrent to participation. The complexity of student funding was found to impede entry and made the interpretation of information difficult, especially for older, low income students with dependents. Forthcoming changes to fees and student funding are likely to further increase the overall complexity of the financial decisions facing HE entrants in England. Metcalf (2005) found that the system of hardship grants had not equalized finances across students. Students in receipt of hardship grants were expecting to incur significantly higher debt than the average (by about a sixth on average) on completion of their studies. However, West et al. (2003) found that the award of a bursary had a positive psychological impact by way of reducing students' fear of debt.

Finance may be perceived not just to influence access to higher education but also the extent to which students are able to persist in HE. Institutional (McCausland et al. 2005) and national (Quinn et al. 2005) data and research suggest that finance is the primary factor causing early withdrawal in relatively few cases. For first generation students in the Quinn et al. (2005) study, poverty was something students had come to expect and learn to live with. However, it did shape decisions such as living at home and working long hours outside of the university, and these often had a strong negative impact. Some research about student bursaries suggests that they have a positive effect on student retention and success. In a small scale study Hatt et al. (2005a, b) found that students at two English HEIs who received bursaries were more likely to successfully complete their first year than non-bursary students from low income backgrounds, and that bursaries eased the transition into HE, favourably altering the students' perception of their university and, for some recipients, their commitment to succeed. Similar findings are reported from an institutional context in Australia (Aitken et al. 2004). Manski (1989) however, has pointed out that the theoretical effect of financial aid on educational outcomes in general, and retention in particular, is ambiguous. By lowering the cost of education, retention is likely to be enhanced, but by encouraging participation among less academically prepared students, financial aid may lower retention and success. Research in the US has failed to reach a consensus on this issue (Kerkvliet and Nowell 2005) and as yet little research has been undertaken in the UK.

The (potential) impact of finance on participation in higher education ʳ students from low income families appears to be straightforward: they ᵗnot afford to enter HE and/or they cannot afford to complete. However ᵃbove discussion indicates that this is a deceptively simple interpretation. ʰer key factor is people's attitude toward debt and, more specifically their ˡe towards getting into debt to fund participation in higher education.

Attitudinal factors are likely to be influenced by parental education, which is discussed in the next section.

Parental education and cultural barriers to access and success

Research demonstrates that family and parents have a very significant impact on educational achievement in school and participation in other forms of learning (Gorard et al. 1999; Gorard et al. 2001). This however raises questions as to which factors are influential – income, occupation, education or location (for example, access to schooling, etc.) For example Gorard et al. (2001) found in their study of lifelong learning in South Wales that the father's occupation and the mother's education and place of birth have the greatest effect on participation in lifelong learning. However, what their interviews illustrate is how important parents' attitudes to school and education are in 'setting an individual on course for a life of learning or its avoidance' (2001: 176). This section of the chapter examines the impact of parental education, and the values this engenders, in relation to child development and achievement, schooling, post-16 and HE decision making, transition into HE and experiences in HE.

Early development and success

Feinstein et al. (2004a, b) used a literature review to examine the effect of parents' education on the development of children, particularly in relation to school achievement. They created a conceptual model of the reasons for the intergenerational transmission of educational success. Their study reviews the impact of a wide range of family characteristics and circumstances and finds that parental education has very significant direct and indirect effects on child development. They acknowledge that this is exploratory research but they suggest that it lays the foundations for future policy development. In the following discussion the model they have developed is explored, and its potential implications for access to, and success in, higher education are considered.

There is a strong and universal relationship between family socioeconomic status (SES) and children's academic achievement (UNICEF 2001). As discussed above, SES or class encompass a range of elements (income, occupation, parental education and locale), but Feinstein (2003) demonstrates that the relationship between social class and attainment, and parental education and attainment is directly comparable, suggesting that parental education is a very important explanatory variable within the broader concept of SES. But, as Feinstein et al. (2004a) and Gorard and Rees (2002) note, other variables such as family structure, income, neighbourhood

or age of mother can also be shown to correlate with attainment. But, crucially, parental education contributes to these characteristics too (Feinstein et al. 2004a). Feinstein et al. show how parental education has a direct role and a mediating affect on other factors affecting child development and schooling success.

Feinstein et al. draw from developmental psychology, and thus move beyond the factors considered in sociology and introduce further variables which have been offered as explanatory in relation to children's development and academic success. They consider the following factors in relation to parental education:

- Family structure, e.g., number of parents, either natural or non-natural, living in the household, marital status, nature of relationship between parents.
- Family size, including number of children in the family, birth order and age differential between children.
- Teenage motherhood and mother's age.
- Income and poverty, including level, timing and duration of poverty.
- Maternal employment, including number of hours and type of employment, and childcare used.
- Parental cognitions, e.g., beliefs, attitudes, aspirations and expectations, interest, values and knowledge.
- Parental mental health and well-being.
- Resources of goods and time, e.g., books, toys.
- Parental physical health.
- Parenting style and parent–child relations, e.g., warmth, discipline, intrusiveness, verbal interaction.
- Educational behaviours, e.g., reading to children, the provision of and engagement in a cognitively stimulating environment, language used.
- Neighbourhood, e.g., local infrastructure, community organizations, characteristics of other residents.
- Pre-school opportunities.
- Schools, e.g., ability grouping, peer group influences, pupil–teacher interactions, teacher expectations.

Feinstein et al. review the empirical and theoretical evidence to consider the impact of each factor on children's development. They also review each of these factors in relation to parental education – for example, what is the impact of parental education, family structure, parental health, etc. This enables the analysis to identify which factors are the most important: how factors draw from parental education to influence child development; and the interaction between factors (Feinstein et al. 2004b).

Following Feinstein et al.'s (2004a) review of each of these factors in relation to parental education (2004a: 21–73) they conclude that parental education can impact on each of these factors directly and indirectly, and it can moderate the negative impact of other factors. For example, parental education affects income; income influences access to resources such as toys

and books etc. But parental education informs which resources are chosen, and thus the negative impact of low income and poverty can be reduced (to some extent) by higher levels of parental education.

Feinstein et al. (2004b) conclude that at the family level parental education and income have a very significant impact on children's attainment. Occupational status is also important, but the channels for the effect of occupation are less clear-cut. Family size is another important factor. Family structure and teen motherhood can have important indirect effects if they occur in combination with other factors, but are not major influences in themselves. Similarly, maternal employment is not a key factor provided quality childcare is available. This is, at least in part, determined by the neighbourhood which also offers access to other experiences, services and schools, which can offset the impact of family level factors in a substantial way. Family characteristics, such as parental well-being and parental beliefs, values, aspirations and attitudes either have independent effects on attainment or are the mechanisms for the effect of socio-demographic factors. Interactions between parents and children, especially parenting skills, can offset or exacerbate the influences of family characteristics and circumstances.

> We find strong theoretical and empirical support for the view that parental education influences most of the factors that have been found to affect children's school attainments. Thus, the role of education is extremely substantial. As well as having a direct influence on most of the key characteristics and parent–child interactions, parental education can also moderate the effects of risk factors and ease the effect of them on interactions between parents and children
>
> (2004b)

This in-depth analysis by Feinstein et al. strongly suggests that parental education is very important in influencing the development of young children, and their success at school. The next section considers the relationship between school success and progression to higher education.

The relationship between school achievement and progression to higher education

Success at school is very important in contributing to participation in higher education and lifelong learning. School shapes people's identities as learners (Gambetta 1987) and provides qualification routes into further learning. As Gorard et al. (2001) note, 'those who are least successful in school are least able to continue, or where barriers are removed are least likely to want to continue' (p.178).

The main determinant of whether or not young people progress into education at the age of 16+ is success in school examinations (Thomas et al.

2001; Croll and Moses 2003; Howieson and Ianelli 2003). Watson and Church (2003) found that potential students from under-represented groups in Year 10 were generally positive (80 percent) about HE, but that many were not likely to reach even the GCSE benchmark usually necessary for sixth form study. Students from families where parents had no formal levels of qualification were less likely to want to stay on (Croll and Moses 2003), although it should be noted that these students also had lower GCSE scores. Research shows that the level of qualification at 16+ predicts very well a student's educational pathway and later employment status (McIntosh 2003). Of the young people who do not stay on at 16, very few (around 4 percent in Raffe et al. 2001) would then return in the second or subsequent years. Of those returning, it is generally the best qualified, with the highest level of parental education and support (Hammer 2003). Thus, 'those who benefit from post-compulsory education, in whatever setting, are those who are already well-educated' (Papadopoulos 2000: 35), or come from families that are well educated.

There is a direct relationship between achievement in post-16 education, and progression to higher education. In the UK, there is currently almost full participation by those qualified to do so, with currently 90% of those students with two or more A-levels progressing to higher education by the time they are 21 (Action on Access 2005). This is perceived to have led to a saturation of the market with traditional middle class A-level students (Abramson and Jones 2004). It should be noted however that only approximately 50 percent of those students with equivalent vocational qualifications progress to HE, and that this is to less prestigious institutions and programmes. Preston's (2004) research found that students from lower socioeconomic groups were guided towards vocational rather than academic qualifications by the post-16 institutions they attended. Socio-economic status was gauged informally by staff, based on students' characteristics, such as the way they behaved – thus pointing to the significance of parental education rather than family income level or other determinants of class. There is therefore a strong link between achievement in secondary schooling, participation in post-16 education and progression to higher education. This is linked to socio-economic status, and is highly likely to be influenced by parental education in particular. Furthermore, in the UK there is a correlation between achievements in post-16 education, and success in higher education: students with higher A-level points scores are more likely to persist and succeed. Statistically, this is not directly related to socio-economic status, but there is a strong relationship between deprivation and a lower average A-level points score (Yorke and Longden 2004: 51), and conversely enrolment in a fee-paying school and a higher average A-level points score (Naylor and Smith 2002).

Schooling not only impacts on qualifications and achievements that facilitate progression into HE, but it shapes the learning identity that people develop – for example, whether or not they perceive themselves as capable learners who should progress to higher education. People's previous learning

experiences impact on their access to higher education (Preece 1999) and their experiences within higher education (Bamber and Tett 2000). In Castles' (2004) study a positive educational experience emerged as one of 12 factors contributing to student persistence in higher education. Donaldson and Graham (1999) argue that earlier learning experiences influence 'learners' motivations, self-esteem, self-confidence, responsibility and intent, as well as . . . the psychosocial and value orientations . . . with which learners approach their education' (p. 29).

There is clear evidence that students from disadvantaged social backgrounds do relatively poorly in the formal education system (Mortimore and Whitty 1999) and that educational disadvantage runs in families (Gregg and Machin 1997; Machin 1998). Gorard (1997) states that the clearest simple indicator of success at school is family background. The importance of parental involvement in schooling has long been recognized (Plowden 1967), however the agency of working class parents is often less than that of middle class parents (Vincent 2001). According to Desforges and Abouchaar (2003), social class, gender, age of pupil and the educational or life experiences of the parent all influence parental involvement. Similarly, McNamara et al. (2000) observe that parental involvement varies enormously depending upon the parent's own educational and life experiences. There are major obstacles that appear to limit parental involvement in schooling and impact negatively on pupils' success in school, and subsequent progression to higher education (Houghton 2005). These factors include negative previous educational experiences, a lack of confidence in supporting their children and a limited understanding of the system (Desforges and Abouchaar 2003).

Transition to higher education

Forsyth and Furlong (2003) found in their study of young people from disadvantaged backgrounds that cultural barriers were implicated in every stage of the decision making process: from whether to stay in post-compulsory education through to which institution and what course to take. In particular, parents play a major role in shaping students' decisions to participate in post-compulsory education (Helmsley-Brown 1999; Moogan et al. 1999; Mangan et al. 2001; Sutton Trust 2002; Archer and Yamashita 2003; McGrath and Millen 2004). Parents also influence students' choice about where to study and what courses to follow (Helmsley-Brown 1999; Brooks 2003, 2004), which are linked to parents' background, with those from higher managerial/professional class backgrounds encouraging participation in HE (Biggart et al. 2004). Reay et al. (2001) note that some of the working class participants appear to be emotionally constrained: they self-excluded themselves from the more traditional universities (see also Forsyth and Furlong 2003) and selected institutions where they felt they could 'fit in' (Leathwood and O'Connell 2003; Read et al. 2003).

Students from families with experience of HE tend to make use of a wide

range of information to inform decisions about which HEIs to attend. For example, they will listen to family and friends, attend open days and use information relating to research and teaching quality assessments (UCAS 2002). Informal advice from families and friends is of variable quality as well as quantity, and this is not compensated for by official advice, support and guidance (Bowl 2001), although different institutions provide different levels and quality of advice. The UCAS (2002) study found that sixth form colleges offered the most support, whereas FE colleges appeared to offer a lower standard of institutional support. Reay et al. (2001) found similar patterns. Private schools offered more intensive careers advice, with a relatively narrow focus pushing towards Oxbridge and other elite institutions. Within non-private schools the career needs of the students were more diverse, including children with special educational needs and those whose parents wanted their children to find work. Further education colleges were found to have a relatively narrow focus in terms of advice and guidance, but aimed at newer HEIs.

Analysis of the literature, and research from the ten countries participating in our study suggests that parental education has a significant impact on determining access to higher education. It is also apparent that it cannot be isolated from other types of disadvantage such as income, occupation and geography. Canadian research (Statistics Canada 2002) shows that parental education is strongly related to income – but further analysis demonstrates that parental education appears to have a stronger influence than family income:

> Of particular interest is the finding that young adults whose parents had post-secondary education [college or university] and fell in the lowest income quartile were more likely to participate in post-secondary education studies themselves, compared with those whose parents were in higher income quartiles but without secondary education

This is demonstrated in Table 5.1.

Similar findings are reported in the US, where Horn and Nunez (2000) compared first generation entrants with their peers whose parents attended

Table 5.1   Post-secondary participation rates for Canadians aged 18–21 and no longer in high school, by household income and parents' education, 1998

Household after-tax income quartile	*Parents' education*	
	At least one parent with post-secondary education (%)	*No parent(s) with post-secondary education (%)*
Lowest	68	48
Lower-middle	76	53
Upper-middle	77	58
Highest	78	56

Source: Statistics Canada 2002

college. The study found that even after controlling for academic achievement, family income, family structure and other related characteristics, first
generation students were less likely to participate in academic programmes
leading to college. This is further supported by examining students who are
highly qualified to progress to HE: those with college educated parents
enrolled at four year institutions at a rate of 16 percentage points higher
than potential first generation college students (92 percent compared to 76
percent) (NCES 1988).

Experience in higher education

At the point of acceptance and entry to HE, research suggests that students
need to develop a sense of entitlement to participate in HE, rather than
seeing this as a privilege (Bamber and Tett 2000; 2001; Tett 2000; Leathwood
and O'Connell 2003). Students from communities where participation in
HE is not the norm feel that they are doing something which is 'breaking the
mould', which may act as a barrier to full engagement with their course of
study. Students who are the first in their family to attend higher education
can feel a lack of entitlement to be there, which may have a negative impact
on their self-confidence.

Once in HE many students from under-represented groups in particular
feel as if they have to learn to 'play the game'. Bowl (2001) describes this
problem in relation to mature minority ethnic students. Hatt and Baxter
(2003) find that students entering HE via vocational routes taker longer to
learn 'the game' than peers entering with A-level qualifications. Forsyth and
Furlong (2003) found that young people had a lack of prior knowledge of
what student life involved. Consequently they were unprepared for the
amount of free time they had and were unsure of how to manage this pro-
ductively. Participants in the UCAS (2002) study expressed similar sentiments and felt they were under-prepared for the transition from 'cosseted
learning style to mass independent HE' (p.30). Evidence of a lack of knowledge of the reality of student life was found in smaller studies of one post-
1992 institution by Leathwood and O'Connell (2003) and another by Read
et al. (2003). Both studies found that non-traditional students (which
included mature, first generation entrants and ethnic minority students) felt
they were expected to be too independent too early and were shocked by
what they felt was a lack of supervision and guidance. Further anxiety was
created by not knowing what was expected in assignments, not knowing how
to structure academic writing, and exam standards (Murphy and Fleming
2000). This lack of knowledge can be viewed as a lack of cultural capital: not
knowing how things are done or what is expected of you. This can be further
compounded for first generation entrants who lack people to ask for this
information – either in their families or social networks.

Wilson (1997) suggests that how students perceive themselves can impact
on the integration process; if they see themselves as being 'different' or as

having special needs this can affect the process of fitting in. The University of California's Undergraduate Experience Survey (UCUES) (University of California 2003) identified some important differences between first generation entrants and other students. In particular, they spent more time studying and preparing for class, more time in paid employment and much less time partying and in other forms of leisure activities. Thomas (2002) found that socialization was an important aspect of integration into a higher education community with positive impacts on academic motivation, willingness to seek help and achievement. Similarly, Forsyth and Furlong (2003) found that students who were unable to find or fit in with other similar students were in danger of becoming socially isolated which ultimately could impact on their confidence and commitment to their course. Social integration can be influenced by both economic factors and cultural ones. For example, participation in activities frequently requires having sufficient disposable income, and living at home (which may be an economic decision) contributes to social isolation (Forsyth and Furlong 2003; Quinn et al. 2005) as there are fewer opportunities to participate in informal and formal social interactions. Shared interests, tastes and values may, however, also enhance social engagement, and conversely different social and cultural backgrounds to the majority may make participation more difficult. Furthermore, students living at home may have different expectations about higher education (Holdsworth and Patiniotis 2004). They tend to see university as an extension of college and have little interest outside of attending lectures. This may be in part because their social networks exist outside of the university, thus the role of social capital may play a role here too. Those students who do seek to become involved in university life can find themselves trapped between two worlds: that of the university where they feel they do not fit in and that of their old community from which they are increasingly being distanced.

Conclusions about the potential impact of parental education

Although parental education is closely linked to social class, educational background has its own significant dimensions, which is why it is a potentially powerful way of examining and implementing the widening of participation. Parental education is a significant determining factor of cultural, social and economic capital for a young person in relation to progressing to HE. But, as discussed in Chapter 4, we do not sufficiently understand what kind of capital a degree constitutes and how it impacts with other forms of capital produced by family networks. In relation to widening participation (access and success), parental educational background is likely to influence:

• Early child development and achievement, including family relationships and values, choices about income expenditure, neighbourhood, peers and schools available, expectations about participation in higher education.

- Achievement in compulsory education through, for example, choice of school, attitude towards learning and support with study.
- Decision to progress to higher education in terms of whether further learning is valued and expected or discouraged, and the extent to which getting into debt to fund higher learning is viewed as an acceptable or appropriate thing to do.
- Providing access to relevant information and advice, and influencing choice of programme and institution, etc.
- Transition and integration in HE, in particular expectations and knowledge about HE, academic skills, identity as a learner, degree of social and cultural similarity and integration with peers, positive or negative support, informed or non-prescriptive support, demands and expectations of the family, living on campus or at home.
- Experiences, knowledge and skills will have been shaped by parents' educational, cultural, social and economic capitals and will mean students bring different interests and perspectives to learning.

These issues will be explored empirically and developed in Chapter 6. A greater understanding of the influence of families, and parental education in particular, will enable the HE sector to respond better to aspirations and realities relating to widening participation. This is likely to involve:

- Greater engagement with whole families – however they are defined – at earlier stages in the educational process.
- Awareness of hidden discrimination that takes place against applicants and entrants from families with no experience of higher education.
- Provision of far better quality and more transparent information on the part of HEIs.
- The development of more effective induction programmes, which provide transparency and clarity about higher education and promote academic and social engagement by all students.
- Development of appropriate curricula that do not privilege prior knowledge, experience and skills of students whose parents are graduates by undervaluing the knowledge, experience and skills of others.
- The adoption of learning, teaching and assessment strategies that favour certain ways of knowing, learning and communicating.
- Overcoming the economic disincentives to studying and tackling the direct and indirect effects of parental background and socio-economic status in the graduate labour market.
- Awareness of the interaction of parental educational background with other equity categories producing multiple disadvantages, needing complex interventions.

6

Empirical exploration of the implications of first generation entry for higher education experiences

Introduction

This chapter draws on the empirical research in the UK with working class and first generation entrants who withdrew from higher education, which we introduced in Chapter 1 and used in Chapter 4. This in depth study allows us to explore the impact of parental education on their higher education experiences and produce a fine-grained account of these processes. The chapter provides an outline of the research study and methods used, which included the utilization of international perspectives. It then focuses on issues faced by first generation entrants in relation to: attitudes towards higher education; applying and entering HE; transition and experiences within HE; and the decision to withdraw from HE. These processes are discussed in relation to parental education, and cultural and social capital, and how these impacted on their experiences and decisions.

Research study

The UK government has pledged that 50 percent of young people (aged under 30) should participate in higher education by 2010, but there is concern that this is being undermined by non-completion, particularly by students from non-traditional groups. It should be noted that non-completion rates have stayed broadly the same since 1992 (Tarleton 2003) and that the UK has high rates of completion in comparison to other OECD countries. Early withdrawal has, however, become an important policy concern.

Higher rates of withdrawal are to be found in many of the post-1992 institutions, which also have greater proportions of students from lower socioeconomic groups (defined by parental employment) and low participation neighbourhoods (based on geography) (see HEFCE 2003). Statistical analysis of the probability of withdrawal for UK university students indicates that non-completion is more probable for students from low ranked occupationally

defined social classes (Smith and Naylor 2001). While this may also be correlated with lower entry grades, it has been interpreted at the national policy level as a concern about 'working class' student drop out. This is not to suggest that students from lower socio-economic groups are less academically capable (Johnston 1997; NAO 2002), but rather it may reflect the impact of earlier educational opportunities and motivations, which in turn can be related to parental education.

Our research study (Quinn et al. 2005) was conducted on behalf of the Joseph Rowntree Foundation. The overall goal of our study was to both understand the meanings and implications of 'voluntary' drop out among working class students under 25, and offer new perspectives and potential solutions. The research involved four post-1992 universities from England, Scotland, Wales and Northern Ireland. All were situated in provincial areas of industrial decline; all recruited strongly among young working class students and provided many sources of support for them; yet all four experienced retention problems, despite the fact that there were few alternative job opportunities locally.

Previous research on drop out has experienced methodological problems. For example, research for the DfES (Davies and Elias 2003) used a postal and telephone survey method to explore student drop out among the student population generally, but this study suffered from a low response rate that led to difficulty in interpreting the findings and doubt about how representative they were. Our methodology attempted to address the shortcomings of previous studies and develop a more appropriate approach to the study of drop out. In exploring the emotive issue of drop out, a different qualitative and participative approach was necessary. Our research sought to maximize participation and attempted to involve ex-students, using a range of qualitative methods. It also strove to set universities and drop out in their local context.

The project began with 'research jury days' at each national location, which were intended to establish a grounded picture of the local and institutional context under study. Each of the four partner institutions hosted an event where the researchers heard evidence from a variety of sources: including working class students still at the university, working class students who had dropped out, lecturers and student support staff, employers, employment agencies, the voluntary sector and representatives from local communities, about what they believed to be the meanings and consequences of drop out. Counterparts of all the speakers, for example, other employers, other lecturers, were also involved in the day, to ask questions and take part in discussion. Working class withdrawal was placed, not in isolation, but in relation to local and national contexts in order that the research team could better understand its impact and implications before proceeding to the interview stage. The research jury days cannot claim to be a totally open method, the research team was making structural choices in whom they invited to speak (and whom they were able to get) and in turn those speakers were gatekeepers for many more perspectives. Since communities are so

diverse there were many voices 'experienced as absences' much as students who have dropped out are said to be. In evaluative discussions following the event the use of the term 'jury' was questioned as setting up connotations of judgement that might prevent some from being willing to take part. However, for others the notion of bearing witness and providing evidence was an important element of the process. The jury days brought together, not only the participants' own stories about drop out, but the stories in currency about others, giving a sense of the cumulative and layering effect of the cultural narrative of working class drop out. Their function was to uncover localized understandings of drop out and to explore the interconnections between the university, work and the community. By bringing together a range of participants who would rarely have entered into dialogue and by carefully structuring that dialogue a wealth of challenging data was generated. In all, the research jury days enabled drop out to be explored and understood in a radically different way (see Quinn 2004a for a full discussion).

The jury days were followed by in depth interviews with working class students under 25 who have dropped out from the four universities. Gaining access to respondents is the persistent problem facing those who want to research students who withdraw. We recognized this from the outset and created the role of participant facilitator in each university to mediate between researchers and participants. These were to be students who had either dropped out themselves or were at risk of doing so. We believed that they would be able to communicate effectively with possible participants and encourage them to take part, using informal networks and contacts to create a snowball effect. In practice the participant facilitators tended to use university data rather than informal means, and in some case were hindered by their personal insecurities engendered by their own experience of dropping out.

Ex-students from the previous five years were identified through institutional data (with varying reliability), and were asked if they were willing to participate in the research. In gathering the interview sample the definition of local, first generation learner was used for students to self-identify as working class. This is clearly not without problems, but using this classification overcomes many of the difficulties of asking students to classify their own socio economic status, while still capturing those who would have been deemed working class by more traditional indicators. We understand 'working class' to be a highly heterogeneous category and the sample was, as expected, rich and diverse. One of the benefits of this approach was that we created a sample of 67 first generation students aged under 25 whom we were able to interview in depth about their HE experiences, of these 40 were young men and 27 young women.

A semi-structured interview schedule was used, including questions about parental education, parental attitudes to higher education; levels of support provided by parents; the influence of entry to higher education on family dynamics; and the impact of dropping out. Interviews were either conducted

face to face, or by telephone. The initial intention was for all interviews to be face to face, however, many ex-students did not turn up for the appointments made by the facilitators. Further interviews were conducted by telephone but contact also proved to be problematic and required some persistence on the part of the researchers. Despite some of the limitations of telephone interviews, the research team concluded that they were sometimes more realistic than expecting ex-students to return to a university from which they had withdrawn. Interviews lasted between 30 minutes and in excess of one hour. While more than 20 interviews were conducted in each institution, a total of 67 were used in the analysis, as the rest did not fit the research criteria (for example, age, class and enrolment status, as discussed above). All interviews were audio-recorded and transcribed. They were then coded both inductively and deductively by the research team, using NVivo software. In addition, the findings of both strands of the research were interrogated in an international participative colloquium involving researchers, practitioners and policy makers from the UK and abroad. The colloquium also considered a set of specially commissioned international research papers exploring how drop out was understood in other countries. The issue of flexibility and return to study emerged as particularly important. Consequently we completed the study by changing our proposed interviews with employers to interviews with university careers and employment services and also conducted a small survey of those knowledgeable about university admissions processes. The findings discussed in this chapter relate primarily to the interviews with first generation students, who have been given pseudonyms, and also draw on some relevant data from the research jury days.

Why students leave higher education and the impact of first generation entry

Until recently, very little has been known about the progression routes of early leavers in the UK. This has started to be addressed, for example through the recent study undertaken by the Department of Education and Skills (DfES 2003b). Performance indicator data have been used to make positive or negative judgements about institutions with little knowledge and understanding of why students are leaving and what they progress on to do. This research allowed us to explore the meanings of withdrawal as understood by the students themselves rather than by policy makers or institutions. In keeping with national data and trends, many of the students interviewed left higher education during the first year of study, often during the first semester (77 percent and 40 percent respectively). Although students frequently gave one ostensible reason for their early withdrawal, a combination of factors was commonly involved. The main reasons for withdrawal can be categorized as:

- Inappropriate information to make course choice
- Poor transition to HE
- Unclear academic expectations and lack of guidance
- Insufficient access to support
- Alienation and isolation
- Too many other commitments
- Financial pressures

These issues, and the experience of leaving university, are now explored in relation to first generation entry, parental educational background, social and cultural capital.

Parental education and attitudes towards higher education

As discussed in Chapter 4, family is a fluid construct. Our participants were expectedly heterogeneous, coming from a range of family structures: including families with two parents, single parent families, step-families, families headed by elder siblings, families where both parents lived outside the household, and they often interpreted family in terms of extended networks of relations. All but a very small number were white families and whiteness is an important aspect of the study which we have discussed elsewhere (Quinn et al. 2006). For all those students in our sample, parents had not had the opportunity of university education: 'back then when my parents were in education they never really had the opportunity to go, it was straight into a job and that was it' (Steve, England).

> Int.: Were you the first person in your family to go to university?
> Alan: Yes out of my immediate family. Mum and dad didn't go to university. Most went straight to work and moved up from there. I think I was even the first to go into further education.
> (Alan, Scotland)

A few participants had elder siblings who had studied for degrees. Some of these siblings had also dropped out, perhaps setting a precedent that 'this is the sort of thing we do'.

Although going to higher education had become far more normalized than it would once have been ('it seems like everybody is going to university at some point or another') their communities were perceived as educationally disadvantaged and still strongly oriented to traditional industries, even in a time of decline: 'I think the education is not as good as it could be you know. I think the people are smart, plenty more could do good. The community I grew up in was more to get a job and stuff' (Paul, Northern Ireland).

It was by no means a foregone conclusion within families that their children would study at university:

Int.: Within the family was it always assumed that you would go through
       the whole education process and end up at university?
Ian: No.

(Ian, Wales)

Although a deficit model of widening participation suggests that such families characteristically lack aspiration (see further discussion in Chapter 7)
and therefore their sights need to be raised by initiatives developed 'for'
them, our research challenges such interpretations. Our participants over-
whelmingly reported their family's attitudes to higher education as positive,
and university as representing a goal that they urged them to reach:

Int.:   What do your mum and dad do?
Pete: Dad is an electrician and mum is a nursery nurse.
        What do you think your family's attitude towards education is?
Pete: They encouraged me, they are trying to get me to go back to
        university now.
Int.:   Why do you think they are so keen, what do they think it will do
        for you?
Pete: They think it will make me go further, give me more opportuni-
        ties job wise? My granddad says if I finish my degree I can be
        anything. I could pack shelves if I wanted to, I can have the
        choice. Whereas, if I don't do my course I won't have a choice.
        You can go down but I can't go up.

(Pete, England)

However, while the discourse of aspiration raising tends to ignore structural constraints, parents did not have that luxury and were very aware of the
limits placed on the family by poverty and class. Of necessity, study had to be
accompanied by paid work so that the family could survive financially. Moreover, study needed to be related to ultimate employment opportunities,
because otherwise both children and family would be placed at risk. Parents
were highly aware of the limited job opportunities in their local area and
while education was seen as a means of gaining advantage, this was by no
means guaranteed. Many of the trappings that surround university education
when it is seen as a process of self-actualization, such as living far away from
home or taking a gap year between school and degree, were not considered
options. Instead university was placed within a web of family imperatives and
as playing an ambivalent role: both potentially protecting family survival and
threatening it. This process appeared to be quite gendered so that it was
young men whom parents most wanted to go to university but whom they
most feared would be lazy, weak and vulnerable to drop out (see Quinn et al.
2006 for an in depth discussion). As discussed in Chapter 4, mothers sometimes drew on memories of their own classed and gendered educational
history to encourage young women to grab education while they still had
a chance: 'Well I did quite want to go to university, but I wanted to go to
college first to do an art course for a year and unfortunately my mother kind

of forced me to go to university; she didn't want me to miss out on the opportunities she'd missed only because she got married instead of going to college' (Anna, Wales).

In many respects the type of higher education these students experienced, its meanings and connotations, were actively shaped by their parents. Emphasis has been placed on the controlling role of middle class parents in negotiating education markets (see Reay et al. 2005) and perhaps working class parents have been positioned as rather hapless bystanders. While it is true that differences in power and resources often restrict their options to intervene, as we shall discuss in this chapter, they are far from passive. They construct a vision of higher education as serving the purposes of their families and those purposes appear to be rather different than those of middle class families. As discussed in Chapter 4, middle class families have been active in protecting their educational capital and holding onto the advantages they already have. Part of this is a belief in the primacy of the educated self, so that being educated is a crucial subject position. For the families in our study a discourse of mobility was important and terms like 'working up' and 'moving up' were often used. Yet it was no longer axiomatic that education was the ladder used to progress to a higher position, nor was it assumed that this 'better' position would be middle class in character. Parents were often described as having a 'working attitude' and this was the dominant factor in their approach to life and to university: 'They didn't really mind what I did as long as I wasn't sitting around the house doing nothing. If I was doing something with my life they were happy enough supporting me' (Greg, Northern Ireland).

This 'working attitude', was not necessarily anti-intellectual and might include auto-didacticism: 'you don't have to have a degree to be intelligent, do you, my father is a highly intelligent man and he'd read all the classics and he'd be constantly learning'. These family dispositions to 'do' rather than to 'be' are highly formative in the educational trajectory of first generation entrants. As we shall discuss they produce possibilities for a more flexible higher education, as well as placing restrictions on capacity to benefit from the existing system.

Applying to and entering higher education

Our research found that once students had made the move to apply for and enter university many felt that they were on the wrong course or programme of study, and this was given as their main reason for leaving. Almost without exception, students felt that they had made poorly informed subject choices. The process of choosing a university and a course was 'rushed' and left many leafing through a prospectus with no real sense of what they should be looking for other than they thought it would be 'interesting'. However, with little guidance from family or institution on what to look for the reality of the course often proved different to expectations. Other students had chosen a

course that they thought, or were advised, would be relatively 'loose' in the sense of providing a wider choice of job options. However, once on the course they failed to see any link with a future career.

These students were disadvantaged by having less access to parental cultural capital to help them inform their choices, and less linking social capital to gain further information from institutions. For example, young people from more middle class backgrounds can call upon well informed parental input in relation to course choice, and are able use networks to find out more information about programmes of study and what others studying similar courses have thought about the experience (see Reay et al. 2005). Working class students had not had the opportunity to develop those tools of self-assessment which are often well honed in a middle class environment and which enable students to place themselves effectively and reap the benefits. Working class students tended to rely on the information provided in the prospectus, rather than to seek information from additional sources, even when the contents were vague:

> I didn't really know what I was going into because the prospectus didn't really give me that much of a clue. I knew it was a new course but I just feel that if they had told me what the exact things were then maybe I wouldn't have picked it
>
> (Claire, Wales)

> The first real experience you have of seeing what is done course-wise is when you actually start university. At the Open Days there are no real examples of work to show you . . . Whenever people go on Open Days from school they're just happy to be out of school and they don't really know what to ask.
>
> (Sarah, Scotland)

> To be perfectly honest, I think it was as much my fault as anybody giving me advice. Looking back now I should have certainly looked into the course and seen what was there . . . I was a bit gullible . . . When I got there I didn't really know what was involved in the course, sociology and psychology and things like that, which I wasn't really too interested in.
>
> (Peter, England)

Many students attending their local institutions, chose the institution first, and the course second because other alternatives such as 'studying down South' were not considered sustainable for the family. Thus, it could be poorly suited to their interests, aptitude and aspirations. For example:

> Initially, I wanted to do HND in computing. I looked at the degree course and I thought it would be too difficult for me . . . When I first spoke to the university they told me the HND course was running, when I came to sign they announced that this course is no longer available.

They then told me about this computer science course. I had only put one option on my UCAS, so then I panicked because I had everything set up for going. I knew it was an opportunity to get more education and I decided to go for it. Looking back at it now, it definitely was too much. A HND would have been much better. When the university told me that it wouldn't be available I should have looked for other options instead: I just panicked and did the degree.

(Michael, Northern Ireland)

In such examples, a lack of access to information and guidance is accompanied by a desire to study near to home, which appears to be much stronger in first generation students than middle class students whose parents have had a traditional higher education experience, which involved moving away.

Poor course choice has a negative impact on the level of commitment and motivation students felt for their programme of study. Some students were unsure of their choice even before they arrived at university, and this impacted on their settling in process, both academically and socially. For others the realization was more gradual: as they gained more knowledge of what the course entailed they saw that either it had little relationship to a future career or that they had little interest in much of the subject matter. 'I just wasn't happy. I felt I was just wasting my life. There was no point in me just sitting there and getting into more debt when I could be at home working . . . I made up my mind at that stage that I wanted to study architectural technology instead'. (Noel, Northern Ireland).

When students did realize that they were on the wrong course, many did not enquire about other options, such as switching programmes because they were unaware that other options existed. Rather, they seemed to feel that they had made their choices and either had to stick with the consequences or withdraw. This again can be contrasted with students who have access to greater knowledge about how higher education operates and a greater sense of entitlement as 'consumers', who would push for a course transfer or complain about the poor match between information provided and the programme being delivered. Students mirrored their parents' lack of confidence in dealing with the system: 'My parents aren't very confident either and you kind of, you know, it rubs off doesn't it'. Tutors did not necessarily encourage these first generation entrants to adopt the mores of their more assertive middle class peers:

It was a case of it's your course, you picked it and you are in it.

(Michael, Northern Ireland)

I went to see my course tutor, I had tears. He just seemed to think it would be better for me to go.

(Marie, Scotland)

Experiences within HE

The transition from school or college to university was problematic for many students. Students with little or no family or peer experience of HE did not seem to know what to expect, how to manage their time and workloads, and often they felt lost and out of control. Even students who had attended a summer school to familiarize young people with their local university found the transition difficult, as the experience was so different to their previous education environment:

> We weren't prepared for the transition between school and university and I went to a thing called a summer school in there as well. We were in a group of about 16 people, and I thought it's all right it is just like school. That gives you a false impression, the fact that you were in a small class and you had a teacher and then when I went to university there were 300 of us sitting in a lecture hall.
>
> (Laura, Scotland)

A number of factors were implicated in this. The combination of an increased workload and more freedom offered the opportunity to 'cop out' and fall behind. Students who felt they had 'coasted through' school and college suddenly experienced difficulties at university. Not only was this unexpected, the experience severely dented their confidence in their ability to progress onto subsequent years of their degree course. This was frequently experienced as an increasing sense of loss of control:

> Int.: What sort of things led up to you leaving, what sort of triggered it off?
> Tom: No support, too much of a heavy workload, thinking that I was losing control in everything that I was studying . . .
>
> (Tom, Wales)

Loss of confidence can also impact on a student's willingness or even ability to seek support, as discussed below.

The change in teaching and learning involved in the transition from school or college to university proved problematic for many. Particular issues included:

- Different learning and teaching styles and methods
- More 'adult' teaching and reliance on independent learning
- Large classes and not enough emphasis on interactive and practical work
- More distant relationships with staff
- Inability to ask for help
- Lack of formative assessment and feedback about progress

Students found it difficult to adjust to the new teaching methods of higher education. For example, they were unsure of whether to listen or take notes during lectures, or how to structure and plan their work.

They just talk. That's about it, it's a lecture, you listen and take notes. When you take notes you forget what they are saying. When you go back to your notes you wonder what you have written down. You don't know whether to take notes or listen.

(Lara, Wales)

. . . the language they used and the structure of the teaching was a lot more in-depth and complicated, it felt a lot more adult

(Leonard, England)

Some students also struggled with the fact that the teaching was not interactive or based on action: 'It would have been useful to work on the computers while the lecturer taught us' (Colleen, Northern Ireland).

Although students were forewarned that the HE environment would be different to that of school or college, for many the change was much more pronounced than expected:

Basically the lecturers gave you the work, if you didn't do it then that was your loss. That was the hardest thing to get used to . . . In terms of doing the work yourself it was a lot harder because nobody encouraged you to do the work. You just got kicked out if you didn't do the work, so it was your loss.

(Pete, England)

Some students struggled academically to make the transition into HE, even if they had been successful in school. This could be related to the learning and teaching styles, or the course contents. Some found the programme was not what they expected, and others found the curriculum contents challenging (especially courses which included maths). Students struggling in their first year frequently assessed their position and decided that they would be unable to cope with higher level academic work in subsequent years. In this situation, continuation represented a further waste of time or renewed/increased effort that they felt unable to sustain.

The course was really hard. I'd do my assignments and I was struggling. I went to the library and worked away, but I just found that no matter how much I studied I just couldn't get my head around it. It was too hard. I wouldn't be able to carry on. I just started to ask myself questions about continuing. I really studied hard but it didn't seem to make much difference. I would never get top marks.

(Lucy, England)

Students entering university from FE into the third year of their degree course appeared to find the transition particularly problematic. While some lecturers were aware of the difficulties this involved and took steps to facilitate students' integration, others were less considerate.

I think he understood that most people come from college and there

were differences in the way people were taught. He advised us how to go about taking notes and then looking at his notes. I found that very helpful. Other lecturers didn't go about it that way.

(Shona, Scotland)

Students experienced difficulties adjusting to the larger class sizes that are typical in many first year programmes. The experience engendered feelings of 'being lost' and 'faceless'; in direct contrast to the college environment many students had previously experienced. Furthermore, the high student to staff ratio restricted their ability to ask questions in the lecture and to approach lecturers for clarification after the class had finished:

They mixed classes, there was music technology and sound technology, and we were all together and there was just too big a group to have a more personal tutoring

(Martin, Scotland)

At university you have large groups, lots of people in one lecture. At college there are only about 25 people and you all get to know each other. The lecturer knows you. Everything is fine. Here the lecturer doesn't even know if you walk past him. He doesn't even know if you are a student. It makes it hard.

(Amy, England)

I found I could never really talk to the lecturers, there were so many people in our class. The lecturers were always busy doing something else. They never had time. There was always someone else talking to them.

(Callum, Northern Ireland)

There were lots of people in the lectures. It was hard to speak to the lecturers. If I had any problems it was hard to get them sorted. The classes were just so big.

(Declan, Northern Ireland)

This anonymity meant that many students felt that they didn't really have any relationship with teaching staff at all. Teaching staff were often perceived as 'unapproachable' and uninterested in students, whose names they did not know. Students experienced further difficulties in making contact with teaching staff outside of lectures, especially, as was true in most cases, if they were living at home and/or had significant part-time employment commitments, as they were restricted in their ability to wait around on campus to see teaching staff. E-learning and online information systems seemed to increase feelings of alienation in new students who are unsure if they were accessing the correct information during a period frequently perceived as 'rushed' and confusing.

The teaching methods: I was used to having close relationships with teachers and lecturers, but in Irish University it was more distant.

(Herbert, Northern Ireland)

I didn't feel comfortable approaching lecturers and asking how I did some of the work. I didn't want to feel like an idiot.

(Phil, Northern Ireland)

Students struggled to access academic support from teaching staff, and they were often unaware of other support (academic and pastoral) that was available elsewhere in the institutions. Furthermore they were reluctant to avail themselves of it. They did not see themselves as the type of person the service was intended for, or felt embarrassment, shame and fear of 'looking like an idiot'. Students who felt they lacked any relationship with teaching staff also tended to contact administrative staff to tell them they were thinking of leaving. This meant they were simply instructed on the technicalities of leaving rather than offered support.

Given the difficulties students found adjusting to the learning and teaching approaches in higher education, and that the environment often made it difficult for them to approach academic and support staff for further information, clarification and guidance, effective formative assessment would have assisted them. However, this too was lacking. This resulted in a lack of academic 'fit' between students and institutions, which was reinforced or exacerbated by a lack of social fit. Developing a sense of belonging within an institution is clearly implicated in student retention (Thomas 2002). Even new universities can be perceived as alien and middle class, while at the same time not inspiring great respect among working class students. For local students in particular familiarity may breed contempt. Establishing a level of social 'fit' proved to be problematic for many of the students involved in the research. Universities were defined by one student as, 'A place for people to meet, where friendships are made'. Developing new friendships facilitates integration and peer support can be a key factor in a student's decision to continue studying or withdraw. But students living at home, and from different socio-cultural backgrounds, often found integration more difficult: 'I had to live at home. The people who lived in the university were part of the environment, whereas I felt like a bit of an outsider. Even though I live round here and it was my town' (Joanne, England). Large classes and didactic, non-interactive teaching methods mitigated against the development of peer-networks in the classroom. In addition, students who felt that they were on the wrong course, or for other reasons had lower levels of commitment to studying, were less willing to commit to making new friends and actively engaging in social activities.

Living in student halls of residence offers opportunities for social engagement which are not available to commuting students. Furthermore, for students not living on or near the campus, participation in social activities is more problematic and this can be further constrained by family and

employment commitments. While some students who remained living in the family home expressed less desire to be involved in the social side of university, others regretted that they had been unable to move away to university, feeling that they had missed out on the 'real' student experience. Some spoke of a making a friend rather than friends, having meals alone and the difficulty of becoming part of a group.

Local students and part-time students are in theory able to access support from their existing friendship groups and family. In reality, this may not always be the case. Students whose friends have not entered HE may find that withdrawing confirms expectations in that 'all my mates were expecting me to quit anyway'. Students whose old friends had also gone to university may be reluctant to discuss problems they are experiencing personally because, 'They [their friends] had done it and they succeeded. I didn't mention that I was struggling with the course or even talk about my thoughts of leaving'. Alternatively, relationships with old friends may suffer due to lack of contact: 'the friendships went downhill because I was never with them'.

In addition to the challenges relating to academic and social integration, students often had to deal with 'non-university commitments', which include both practical time consuming responsibilities such as caring for family members or taking paid employment, and social and emotional commitments. The latter could be as weighty or have similar negative impacts on continuation as more visible pressures. Furthermore, it is not always the simple existence or lack of particular social relations that can support or inhibit continuation. Rather, it may be access to those relations at key times during the student experience. 'Sometimes, when I did the foundation course I didn't enjoy it, but then I'd go back to my room and I'd have a laugh with my mates again. When I wasn't living in halls and I had a bad lesson I'd just mope around for five hours until my next lecture' (Naill, Northern Ireland).

In terms of the practical and emotional commitment to employment, the experience of students could be complex. Not all students worked in paid employment during their studies, but those who did, framed it in one of two ways. On the one hand there was talk of this being an energy and time-sapping strain, on the other hand simultaneous study and employment could be experienced as a positive – albeit not sustained – approach to university life. In this sense employment could open up alternative friendship circles, or simply provide more stimulating and satisfying experiences. Consequently, at the time of dropping out, employment could provide support in preventing the individual from suddenly facing a great gap where study once was:

Int.:   Were you working? Was that a commitment?

Karen: Yes. I had a part-time job in Safeway – just working in the cash office. It got to the stage that when I wasn't going to university so much I did more hours at Safeway just to cover the day. I wasn't even turning up for university towards the end.

(Karen, England)

In the case above, the experience seems a gradual drift into employment as a practical inverse of the drift from university. This is an indication of the sometimes limited personal investment that some students have in attending university. Where an activity is entered into half-heartedly it is not surprising that its loss would not be immediately felt and its replacement would be easily met. At times, full-time employment is entered at the point of drop out simply because it is there.

It is interesting that students expected participating in higher education to be a financial struggle and this seemed to be implicitly accepted. Many of the students lived in families where money problems were the norm and daily life was precarious. As discussed in Chapter 4, students saw themselves as having moral responsibilities to the family and as a contributing to its shared resources as both student and worker:

> . . . at the time my Mum and Dad were running a public house and she went off with the guy who used to come in the pub and they split up. My Dad kept hold of the public house, but it was making no money, so I went to university as expected, and I was working in the pub as well . . . running the pub at night going to university, there wasn't a lot of staff because of the money. Because of the money situation my father went back to full-time work, it was shift work as well so he wasn't there and I was just 18 so I was doing lectures but not all of the work
>
> (Carl, England)

Students rarely identified finance as the explicit reason for their withdrawal, even though having to support themselves clearly contributed to the pressures they faced and having to ask parents for money they could not afford was particularly hard:

> . . . it wasn't them that chose for me to go to university, it was me that chose to go out there and do it, so why should they be punished and that is what I felt like I was doing, I was punishing them because of the amount of money that was getting spent on me just in travelling alone, never mind give me money maybe for food
>
> (Alan, Scotland)

Students worked hard and experienced a severe shortage of time, with often negative consequences for their studying:

> John: I was going to university in the day, like the normal 9–5 hours, the normal studying hours and then I was working in like bars in the evenings from 7pm onwards.
> Int.:   Was that every night of the week?
> John: Yes
> Int.:   Weekends are well?
> John: Yes I usually had Sunday morning off
>
> (John, England)

> . . . at one stage I was doing too much part-time work along with my uni

course, but I probably needed telling to give up one of your part-time jobs, you are here to do your university course – if this is what you want, I just wanted a shove in the right direction . . . it got to one point where I was doing like 37 hours a week over Christmas. With a full-time course as well I had got two part-time jobs. I just needed telling, do you know what I mean. I just wanted that support, for someone to say you are here to do your uni course

(Helen, Wales)

Despite these challenges students faced in higher education, all of the students we interviewed argued that their parents had supported them while they were at university. This ranged from the practical support in providing a roof over their head and financial subsidy, to emotional support and even attempts at academic support:

Int.:   Were your family interested in what you were doing at university? Did they ask you about it?
Pete: Yes, they didn't understand a lot of it but they were keen to try
Int.:   Do you feel they supported you while you were there?
Pete: Yes they tried to help me when I was stuck or if I needed any help. Again they didn't really understand it.

(Pete, England)

Parents were interested and actively engaged: 'both my parents have always asked what is going on, they are quite nosy'. As the majority of our participants lived at home during their studies, for reasons of finance, convenience or security, being at university became an everyday part of the family experience and absorbed into the rhythms of family life. Many subsequently perceived this as a problem: living at home prevented them from fully engaging in university: 'it was too easy just to come home' and the 'comfort' of home became a 'hindrance'. Relationships within the family were reciprocal with students providing sources of support for parents as well as benefiting from their help: 'My mum and dad are both disabled so I would have preferred to stay close. My mum doesn't keep that well and sometimes she has quite bad turns, so I would rather be there in case I needed to do something' (Marie, Scotland).

As discussed earlier, there were also high levels of parental anxiety about whether the family investment was going to pay dividends, and a sense of insecurity about what a degree could realistically offer. As argued in Chapter 4, parents occupied an ambivalent position and could see-saw in their responses to their child's education.

Leaving higher education

Contrary to popular notions of student withdrawal, the majority of students in our study made a thoughtful and rational decision to leave HE, while only

a minority drifted away. Student drift is the gradual process by which some students' engagement with a university will end. This is typically understood in terms of waning attendance at lectures, seminars and so on, that is often not recognized or commented on by the HEI staff:

> It had been building up for some time. I gradually started to go to classes less and less. There would be weeks that I didn't go, then I would turn up, speak to people say I was embarrassed because I hadn't gone. Eventually, after the half-term break I just didn't go back
>
> (Marie, Scotland)

Int:　Tell me about the process by which you left?
Noel:　It was gradual and my attendance dwindled out. It wasn't an abrupt end, it was gradual. I started thinking about the options, as I attended some of the classes my mind became more made up and I realized it wasn't for me.

> (Noel, Northern Ireland)

Thus, for some students drop out was a non-choice, in that they drifted into it or initiated it rather than do exams or assignments they felt they would fail. However, for the majority of students in our study it can be perceived as a rational decision in response to a set of circumstances which made study at that time and place unproductive for them. They made active decisions, which they did not take lightly:

> I didn't find it an easy decision. I took lots of things into consideration. I didn't want to stay just for my friends. I wanted to do what was right from myself
>
> (Elaine, England)

> In a sense I feel I have let myself down. In another, I feel I have been a bit brave in deciding it wasn't for me and that I wanted to do something else and not waste time
>
> (Debbie, Wales)

However, because of the way withdrawal was managed by institutions and presented to students as a dead end, withdrawing was largely experienced as disempowering. This was true even when it was simultaneously a relief, 'a burden taken off my back'. Choosing to leave early became dropping out with all its connotations of fecklessness and failure. However, withdrawing can also be seen as a learning experience. With hindsight, participants were now aware of what they *should* have done at the time: such as choosing a course more carefully; finding out more detailed information on course content; being more aware of less explicit information contained within a prospectus; joining clubs or societies, and seeking specific help or advice and guidance. This starts to indicate how first generation entrants were disadvantaged in relation to their choices and experiences in HE as they lacked 'insider knowledge' about how to access appropriate information, what to

expect in higher education and how to change courses or institutions – knowledge which middle class students have access to through their families and friends. The majority of students feel they have learnt from their higher education experience and will be better equipped next time.

The majority of students who had withdrawn believed that they would return to higher education and operationalize the knowledge they gained from entering higher education and leaving early. Indeed, 20 of the 67 students had either already returned to HE or had serious plans to do so in the near future, while many others envisaged a university education as playing a role in their future and only one said they would never want to return to university again. Thus, rather than being serial 'failures' they would be well equipped to make the most of future university opportunities.

In the process of leaving, hardly any students turned to university support services for help, but many did turn to their parents. On one level this is unsurprising, but on another it indicates that despite their parents' lack of knowledge of universities, they were still trusted to give the right guidance. Despite showing signs of disappointment, few parents attempted to persuade them to stay, even when 'they were a bit gutted about it' or experienced it as a loss of face within their community: 'It was the pride thing, like one of his children had gone to university and I think he had told his friends about this and he was so proud, but when I left, it was like I had let him down almost' (David, Scotland). The overwhelming response, repeated in virtually every interview was that they wanted their children to be 'happy' and to 'do what they wanted to do' and a degree seemed incidental rather than essential to that:

Int.:   When you were leaving university how did your family react to your decision. Did you talk it over with them?

Alan: They left it up to me. They said if I wasn't happy there was no point in staying. They would support me whatever I did. They said not to quit just for the sake of it. They kept telling me that I needed to be sure it was the right decision. They couldn't make it for me. It had to be my decision, but they would support my decision whatever it was

(Alan, Scotland)

They are pretty broad minded. Mum was really pleased when I said I wanted to go to university, especially because nobody in our family had been before. When I felt that I wanted to leave university I told my Mum. She said if I wasn't happy I should just do what I wanted to do

(Nathalie, England)

Flexibility and contingency were the hallmarks of parental responses, perhaps because they knew from experience that life could be lived quite well without a degree: 'obviously they haven't been to university and they have got on with life and everything without a degree'. Although commonly presented as a life disaster, for our participants withdrawing early was a rational

decision, as we have discussed. Furthermore, as discussed in Chapter 4, it can even be seen as a bid for more flexible lifelong learning as they saw themselves returning in the future, studying different subjects and different types of courses and sought a system which was much more fluid than the one they had experienced the first time. Through their lack of rigidity, parents of first generation entrants played a hitherto unacknowledged role in setting this flexible agenda.

International papers which we commissioned as part of the study confirm that such greater flexibility is certainly possible. For example, in Canada 'to be classified as having dropped out a students must be absent for more than six consecutive semesters' (Bonin 2004: 4) and longer periods of non-studying are also allowed in European countries such as Germany. In Australia the distinction between full-time and part-time study is becoming increasingly blurred (Heagney 2006) and Croatia is actively restructuring its HE system around the concepts of lifelong learning and the learning society (Vidacek-Hains 2003). While we are not suggesting that any of these national systems have found perfect solutions to the issue of first generation entry and early withdrawal they point to the possibility of constructive change.

Conclusions

Parental education affects attitudes towards HE, the process of deciding to apply and enter higher education, transition, learning and teaching, social engagement and integration, and the decision to leave higher education. At all of these stages in the students' lifecycle, parents of first generation entrants can be perceived as supportive of their students, but the support tends to be non-directive and non-prescriptive. Parents appear to be broadly in favour of higher education and to encourage their children to participate, but they can only provide limited guidance about which courses or institutions to attend. Here, practical issues may serve as limiting factors, for example: the perceived relationship between the course of study and subsequent employment; or proximity of the institution to home. Parents who have not been to higher education themselves are less aware or are unaware of the nuances of the HE sector, for example: the relationship between institutional type and/or subject studied and graduate employment opportunities and salaries (Pitcher and Purcell 1998; Brown and Hesketh 2003).

Students from non-traditional backgrounds have access to more limited information from their families and friends (see also Bowl 2001), and make use of a narrower range of official sources of information (UCAS 2002). For example, these students are less likely to access and utilize information that is publicly available about individual HEIs, which might include teaching quality and research assessments, employability data, completion rates, etc. These sources of information are more likely to be used by applicants from higher social classes (UCAS 2002). With hindsight students felt they should have made use of a wider range of information rather than relying on

prospectuses and visits, but often practical considerations overrode these factors when the applied initially. Connor et al. (1999) suggested a number of ways in which the quality and scope of information provided to applicants could be improved, and which would have particular benefits for students who do not automatically know what information is available and how to access it. For example, they suggest developing a checklist of the types of information that might be looked for; a comprehensive guide to sources of information and how they might assist with pre-entry decision making; and a single point of contact with institutions where potential students can find information on, and discuss, all issues of concern for them.

The transition into higher education is similarly marked by less knowledge than that of peers who have come from families, schools and communities with a history of participation in higher education. Even students who have participated in pre-entry interventions find that the transition to HE is challenging both academically and socially. This is reinforced further by lower levels of self-confidence that seem to exist, and which result in a reluctance to ask for clarification from teaching staff. Personal circumstances, such as living at home, caring commitments and part-time employment, reduce many first generation entrants' opportunities for social interaction. This has a negative impact on students' sense of engagement, identity and belonging in higher education, and reduces the level of peer support that can be drawn upon to ease the transition into HE. These students also appear to be less willing to access academic or pastoral support from formal support services. A lack of confidence about academic abilities and genuine academic struggle were often accompanied by challenging circumstances, such as family responsibilities, concern about money, high levels of part-time employment and/or a significant commute to attend lectures and seminars. Thus, it is not surprising that students did not identify a single factor that prompted them to leave, but rather it was the combination of circumstances and the lack of alternative options that were open to them. Many of these students felt that they had to decide to stay or leave, rather than to negotiate a change in their situation. For example, students left (and sometimes applied to re-enter) HE, rather than switching to a part-time mode of study, changing their programme of study, taking a semester out for extenuating circumstances or transferring to another institution. Students with access to greater social and cultural capital, which can be understood as more knowledge of the higher education system, are more likely to have negotiated one or more of these alternatives if they needed to.

Leaving higher education was not a decision taken lightly by the majority of our students, and many wanted to re-enter HE at some future point. Parents were often disappointed about these decisions, but again were supportive. This may also be in contrast to parents who have experienced higher education themselves, who may be able to provide reassurance that things will improve, or suggest a course of action to address the difficulties being faced. These parents, however, seemed to be more concerned about the happiness of their children rather than the goal of achieving a higher

education qualification. They had a more flexible attitude towards university education, seeing it as simply a part of life.

This analysis of first generation students' experiences applying to, entering and leaving higher education shows the complex interplay of social, cultural and economic capital. Financial issues influenced choices of institution and course and shaped their HE experience (including the need to work part-time and in some cases to live at home). However, access to informal 'insider' information, advice and guidance from family and friends has had a profound influence in relation to all stages of the student lifecycle. This suggests the need for systemic and institutional development and change to enable more first generation entrants to prosper in higher education.

7

National and institutional approaches to supporting first generation entrants

Introduction

This chapter explores approaches to supporting first generation entrants to access and succeed in higher education. This includes a discussion about the alternative principles that inform approaches to widening participation, and the implications these have on the interventions that are developed and implemented. The chapter proceeds to examine the different approaches that are being used nationally and by higher education institutions in the countries participating in the international research study.

Alternative approaches to widening participation

Contrasting approaches to widening access and promoting student retention and success can be identified in national and institutional policies and practices, and in the related literature. The particular approach to widening participation which is adopted (either explicitly or implicitly) informs the interventions which are implemented. It is useful to outline three approaches (based on Jones and Thomas 2005) before moving to consider the range of strategies and practices which are used in different countries to support the access and success of first generation entrants.

Academic approach

The first approach to widening participation is described as the 'academic strand of the access discourse' (Jones and Thomas 2005: 616). In summary, this approach assumes that students from under-represented groups have the academic potential to enter and succeed in higher education, but lack

either the aspirations or information to access HE. The academic approach to access (Ball 1990; Williams 1997) tends to explain differential rates of participation on the basis of attitudinal factors, which are distinguished from educative potential. This implies that non-participation should be viewed as a consequence of a lack of expectations or 'low aspirations' (HEFCE 2004). This approach therefore positions the individual, family, or group as inadequate and culpable, a view which is disputed by much of the research about access and widening participation (Preece 1999; Thomas 2001a: 130–9, b; and Archer et al. 2003).

Placing responsibility for non-participation squarely on the shoulders of non-participants tends to excuse the national system and higher education institutions from reform. For example, the structure of higher education, admissions processes and the curriculum remain largely unchanged. Thus, the academic approach to the widening of participation is underpinned by a deficit model of the potential entrant (Griffin 1993), which seems very much akin to 'victim blaming' (Tight 1998) and is unlikely to engage such students (Osler and Starkey 2003: 245). This deficit view of widening participation sees non-participants and students from under-represented groups, especially first generation entrants, as culpable and needing to be changed in order to benefit from higher education. In the broader context of education and training Christine Griffin argues that: '. . . the discourse of education and training constructs working class young people and/or young people of colour as "deficient" in various ways which are assumed to affect their academic performance or their orientation to school' (Griffin 1993: 200).

With regard to access and success in higher education if the 'problem' is constructed in terms of individual failure or deficit (low aspirations, lack of motivation, insufficient preparation for HE and unsupportive family background) the solution therefore lies largely with the individual and attention is diverted from structural and institutional factors that inhibit and constrain access and success. Constructing new student cohorts in this way (as problematic and lacking something) influences the solutions that are devised and implemented: these tend to emphasize remedial solutions to rectify assumed deficiencies (Griffin 2001: 153). The potential contribution of these people to higher education is ignored, and instead they are assumed to require 'fixing' or normalizing. Thus, first generation entrants and working class students in higher education are frequently constructed as both a problem and at risk (of dropping out and 'failing'); see, for example, the recent higher education White Paper (DfES 2003b; see also Griffin 2000; Griffin 2001: 154). Our international analysis, however, demonstrates that students from lower socio-economic groups do not necessarily have lower rates of success in tertiary education (see Chapter 4).

The academic approach tends to give rise to project-based activities, which all too often have a short-term orientation (Woodrow 1998). The stress is on aspiration raising initiatives, aimed at encouraging 'gifted and talented' pupils to continue in post-16 education and to enter higher education. Gifted and talented are defined as 'those young people with the talent to

access universities with the most demanding entry requirements' (DfEE 2000: 16). Additional activities may seek to provide more information about higher education on the assumption that non-participation can also result from a lack of awareness regarding post-school options. In the academic approach, the emphasis is on persuading or attracting already qualified students to enter an unreformed higher education system which offers little or no additional support or understanding to foster students' success within higher education. This approach may be described as 'cream-skimming' (Taylor 2000; Coates and Adnett 2003) as it is basically directed at plucking what are assumed to be anomalous intelligent first generation students from their roots in order to place them in the top universities. Projects are usually located outside of, or on the periphery of, universities and have little or no impact on institutional structures and culture.

The academic strand of the access discourse ignores the complexity and multiplicity of obstacles facing people from lower socio-economic groups, and therefore offers simplistic solutions. This is not to suggest that the provision of improved information about higher education, and encouraging people who may not perceive themselves as learners, is irrelevant. Rather, the approach is limited, as it ignores the structural barriers – such as class and educational background – and may reinforce rather than overcome cultural and socio-economic divisions (see Thomas 2001b; Slack 2003).

In recent years in the UK and many other countries the academic model appears to have informed a significant proportion of government thinking around access to higher education. For example, the Excellence Challenge (DfEE 2000) was an initiative that provided £150 million over three years to encourage disadvantaged young people to study at university. It was premised on the idea that qualified students from lower socio-economic groups required more information and higher aspirations to encourage them to enter higher education, and much of the activity centred on outreach activities coupled with 'opportunity bursaries' (a critique of the Excellence Challenge is presented in Thomas 2001b). A number of countries including Australia, Croatia, England and the US have used institutional scholarships, bursaries and financial aid packages to attract already successful students to study at a particular institution. Such approaches may enable some people from lower income groups to access and remain in higher education, but they do not address the other barriers to participation, or the ways in which social and cultural capital impact on students' higher education experience as discussed in the previous chapter.

Utilitarian approach

The second approach to widening participation is termed the 'utilitarian' strand (Jones and Thomas 2005: 617; see also Williams 1997). This approach may see potential entrants as having low aspirations and insufficient information about higher education opportunities, but it recognizes that academic

credentials may be lacking too. Although this could be described as a 'double deficit' view, proponents do not necessarily perceive non-participants as wholly culpable. The utilitarian perspective focuses on the relationship between the higher education sector and the economy, and the need for the former to adapt to meet the needs of the latter (Ball 1989). From a utilitarian perspective curriculum reform is seen to be essential to improve the economic responsiveness of the HE sector. Notions of employability, plus learning skills and student support modules articulate with this approach, displacing or diluting subject specific content (see e.g. Thomas et al. 2002). Vocationally oriented and work-based programmes may also be offered as new forms of higher education.

This approach may also engage with aspects of the structural barriers confronting non-participants, such as negative educational experiences, poor schooling and low academic achievement, low family income and social and cultural dispositions that may not value study at degree level. But while individual students are not implicitly blamed, they are still required to adapt, although the institution or system may provide support for this process. Typical utilitarian interventions include compensatory pre-entry activities (Thomas 2001), generic skills and employability modules (Thomas and Jones 2006) and means-tested bursaries in an Australian context (Aitken et al. 2004).

Within many UK HEIs currently active in promoting the widening of participation there is a tendency towards the utilitarian approach, particularly among the new universities (Bargh et al. 1994; Scott and Smith 1995), and (to a lesser extent) the lower ranked pre-1992 institutions. This is heavily influenced by the employability agenda and links to the current HEFCE preoccupation with withdrawal, and 'student success'. To date, this strand has had little to say about changing the format and structure of traditional three year full-time degree programmes. Subsequently widening participation initiatives in utilitarian influenced HEIs are more or less 'bolted on' to core work, for example mentoring and guidance activities, learning support mechanisms (via 'study skills centres', etc.) and stand-alone student services. These processes are often not integrated with core activities such as learning and teaching. For example, while research examining student services has identified *some* examples of integrated student support, many student service departments reported institutional resistance to their integration into core activity (Thomas 2002).

In the UK there are numerous examples of widening participation activities at the pre-entry stage which aim to prepare students for higher education. For example, certain HEIs work with first generation entrants to improve their educational aspirations and assist them in the acquisition of academic skills to enhance educational achievement. This is also the aim of the revised Aimhigher scheme, which now includes both raising aspirations and raising achievement in school for young people who would not otherwise proceed to higher education (HEFCE 2004). Accredited summer schools provide pre-entry programmes to enable students who have not achieved the

appropriate entry qualifications at school to 'catch up', prior to admission (Blicharski 1998). In the US the TRIO Program (discussed below) supports access to higher education, the transition process and assists students in HE. However, most of this support is not integrated into the core curriculum, often taking the form of supplementary education.

The utilitarian approach to widening participation does not explicitly blame students for their non-participation, but it still seeks to change students to fit into a higher education system which is serving a broader purpose than meeting learners' needs. Griffin (talking in relation to youth research) argues that the alternative approach is to take the 'perspectives of these working-class young people seriously (although not necessarily at face value)' (Griffin 2001: 150). In a similar vein, the academic and utilitarian approaches to widening participation can be contrasted with a transformative approach (Jones and Thomas 2005: 618–19). This third approach contends that participants should not be required to change *before* they can benefit from higher education, but rather a diversity of experiences is perceived as a strength, and thus higher education should be overhauled to benefit from the new experiences and knowledges that new student cohorts bring with them.

Transformative approach

A transformative approach to widening participation is related to the progressive thinking around adult education, and the more radical precepts of the access movement. It embraces the idea that higher education should change to enable it to both gauge and meet, the needs of under-represented groups. This has much in common with the influential work of Paulo Freire (1972). Rather than being predicated on deficit models of potential entrants, and positioning students as lacking aspirations, information or academic preparation, transformation requires serious and far-reaching structural change (Corrigan 1992), which is informed by under-represented groups and their families and communities (see Preece 1999, Taylor 2000). It is therefore concerned with creating a higher education system and an institutional culture that does not require participants to change before they can benefit from higher education. Furthermore, it perceives diversity as a definite strength (Thomas 2002). Nor is the focus upon creating change via short-term, marginal projects undertaken by a few committed practitioners. Rather, all of an institution's activities are to be underpinned and informed by valuing and learning from difference and diversity. Such an approach requires institutions to review their processes of knowledge production and transfer (Thomas and Jones 2000) and their internal structures of power and decision making (Thomas et al. 2005).

A transformative approach should conceive of curricula partly as a response to the input of new cohorts of learners. It must also encourage critical reflection, together with an understanding of the constructed qualities

of knowledge, and the various implications of this. Moreover, it should attempt to prioritize knowledge that is of value and relevance to under-represented groups (Freire 1972). Stuart (2002) thus envisages '. . . a broader set of literacies that enable people to negotiate their own futures. . . . In all of these, the learner would be developing the language of question-ing, to seek out new ways of understanding our world' (p.120). Similarly, in the context of lifelong learning Jane Thompson (2001) advocates learning that is relevant to people's lives and concerned with personal, social and political change:

> Lifelong learning will be most purposeful when it is related to the ordinary concerns of everyday life, and it is not seen as something that other people do, or which is irrelevant. It will be most engaging when it captures the imagination, encourages emotional involvement and pro-vides for the satisfaction of unfulfilled desires. It will be most sustained when it gets results in the form of palpable personal, social and political changes
>
> (Thompson 2001: 38)

Transformative sentiments are expressed by the University of California:

> The University of California [survey] results suggest that first generation college students at the University of California make a significant posi-tive contribution to the University of California learning environment. In addition to contributing an important element of socio-economic diversity to the student body, the profile of first generation college stu-dents is a very positive one. These are students who report dedicating more of their time to their studies while more likely to be working on or off campus and contributing to community service. First generation students report spending significantly less time 'partying'.
>
> (University of California 2003)

However, examples of a transformative approach within higher education (as opposed to adult education) are, unfortunately, few and far between. One such example, however, is provided by Bland (2001), who identifies the ways in which a group of students from lower socio-economic backgrounds were involved in the students' guild and influenced governance at the Queensland University of Technology, Australia, changing both policies and practices to better support students from non-traditional backgrounds. These students entered the university via an outreach programme, and through the peer support gained from a network of these students, five students were elected to the Guild. Not only did this benefit them personally (through increased confidence, a deeper understanding of politics and enhanced academic achievement), but it permitted them to learn about, question and challenge, the traditional workings of the university, and ultimately to bring about positive change for other students from under-represented groups. Through systemic change the needs of the least advantaged became a normal feature of planning (p. 199).

Institutional implications of alternative approaches to widening participation

The preceding discussion has illustrated that alternative approaches to widening participation are informed by different views about first generation entrants, and students from other non-traditional groups, and this influences views about whether students or institutions/national systems should change, or both, and the type of higher education that should be provided. In addition, these views can shape institutional mission and organizational structure, policies and practices. Recent research in the UK explored institutional responses to widening participation (Thomas et al. 2005). This uncovered the different reasons why widening participation may be undertaken, and the implications this has on the organization and implementation of widening participation. Some widening participation activities are intended to increase participation by students from under-represented groups in higher education per se, while others are intended to boost recruitment to a particular institution (see Murphy 2002). For example, one research intensive university said: 'This activity . . . is done on a general widening participation basis . . . the University does not expect to see increases in the intake of students . . . as a result of programmes like this'. This approach can be contrasted with other institutions which have developed their activities to serve the needs of both students and the institution. For example, one institution has developed new campuses and new courses to bring relevant HE programmes to people in deprived areas with low rates of participation in HE and, at the same time, to boost the institution's recruitment figures. The former approach results in a distance between widening participation and admissions, whereas the latter results in a close or integrated relationship as well as a commitment to improving the students' learning experience within higher education.

Widening participation per se appears to be more altruistic, but it can create sustainability difficulties, as the activity is largely dependent on external or ring-fenced funding streams. When funding ceases there is little or no incentive for the intervention to be continued. This can be contrasted with the situation at other institutions which focus on recruiting students to their programmes: 'The initiative is stable and long term having involved substantial investment in new campus provision. Specifically, the FD/BA (Hons) in Popular Music and Technology continues to recruit strongly and to achieve good outcomes in terms of degree attainment'. A focus on recruitment can be a useful mechanism to encourage institutional change in contrast to a focus on changing students to fit into an unreformed higher education. It shifts the emphasis from outreach to 'in-reach' (Murphy 2002) or from 'collaboration between HEIs to collaboration within' them (Thomas 2002).

The extent to which institutions focus on 'recruitment' or 'altruism' is likely to influence institutional structures. Thomas et al. (2005) identified

two models of organizational structure. The first model is the *dispersed organizational structure*, in which each faculty and service has responsibility for widening participation in addition to their core work. This approach seeks to promote the integration of widening participation into all of the institution's activities. It is, therefore, based on a widening participation for student recruitment model and embraces many aspects of the transformative approach. This model can, however, result in a piecemeal approach, with little or no connection between different activities if the process is not managed. A hybrid model, involving a dispersed organizational structure with centralized coordination can address this problem. For example, at the University of Huddersfield all services and schools have to develop a widening participation strategy, and this process is supported by a widening participation specialist who ensures the plans cover the whole student lifecycle; guards against duplication; facilitates the process of sharing good practice between schools and services; and promotes a coherent and cohesive approach.

A dispersed model of widening participation can be contrasted with a *centralized organizational structure*, where the emphasis is on a 'centre for widening participation' (or similar) that coordinates and promotes widening access across the institution. This provides a focus for widening participation, but it can result in an isolated approach with *only* the centre for widening participation taking responsibility for this issue. This model can be associated with institutions that are not looking to recruit widening participation students themselves, and who are dependent on external project funding for their widening participation activities. Here the emphasis will be on changing and preparing students to enter higher education, rather than on institutional transformation.

National approaches to supporting first generation entrants

This section of the chapter draws heavily from our international study (Thomas and Quinn 2003a) to explore ways in which national and regional governments and higher education systems are promoting the access and success of first generation entrants in higher education. As the study demonstrates, higher education systems are structured differently, and operate in contrasting ways (as discussed in Chapter 2). This is informed by issues such as level of institutional autonomy, national legislation and the primary and high school education systems. Other national factors may also be significant, such as the impact of the Homeland War in Croatia, the geography of the country (such as in Sweden and Canada) and the political party that holds power (as in the current situation in Australia, which can be compared with that of the 1990s).

The study asked participating countries to identify ways in which the regional or national government (as opposed to institutions themselves) were promoting the access and success of first generation entrants. An analysis of

the responses has categorized them into four types of activity: government-led targeting; data collection, evaluation and benchmarking; alternative entry routes; and alternative delivery. These approaches and associated examples are now discussed and considered in relation to the earlier discussion in this chapter – namely the informing principles.

Government-led targeting

Governments in different countries have targeted students from under-represented groups in a range of ways. The international analysis suggests that if a government has a commitment to increasing the participation in higher education of a specific sector of society, it must put in place targeted mechanisms to achieve these goals. A spectrum of approaches, however, can be identified ranging from: outreach and support programmes for students, to institutional change and new institutions. At the former end of the spectrum the emphasis is on students being enabled to fit into an unreformed higher education sector (in other words, an academic approach), while at the latter end the emphasis is on recognizing the limitations of the HE sector and developing better provision. The imperative informing change, however, may be the needs of economy, and/or the needs of students (in other words, a utilitarian or a transformative approach).

Targeted national programmes

In a number of countries the government has developed and supported national programmes that target first generation entrants and other students from lower socio-economic groups to enter higher education and, in some instances, to be successful within higher education. Examples of such interventions are the TRIO Program in the US, and Aimhigher in the UK.

In the US, the federal TRIO Program of activities, initiated in the 1960s, supports students from under-represented groups to improve access, facilitate the transition into higher education, increase retention and improve completion rates. For example, *Talent Search* and *Upward Bound* are focused on improving access and facilitating the transition to higher education, while *Student Support Services* is a college-based retention activity designed to foster baccalaureate completion. By law, the programmes are targeted on low income and first generation students, where low income is defined as 150 percent of the poverty level (currently, about US$28,000 in net taxable income for a family of four), and where first generation is defined as neither parent having completed a bachelor's degree. Today there are seven TRIO programmes serving over 850,000 low income students across the country. The McNair Program is an interesting example, as it is aimed at supporting and encouraging students from disadvantaged backgrounds in continuing at university into doctoral studies.

An estimated two million Americans have graduated from colleges and universities with the support of one or more TRIO Programs since 1965.

However, only one in four American colleges and universities house a TRIO Program, and the Council for Opportunity in Education estimates that the programmes reach only 7 percent of eligible low income Americans. Evaluation studies have shown that students in the Upward Bound Program are four times more likely to earn an undergraduate degree than those students from similar backgrounds who did not participate in TRIO; and nearly 20 percent of all black and Hispanic freshmen who entered college in 1981 received assistance through the TRIO Talent Search or the Educational Opportunity Centers (Allen et al. 2005).

The TRIO Program can be compared to the UK Aimhigher initiative. The integrated Aimhigher programme (DfES 2003b) adopts a collaborative approach, bringing together HE institutions, further education colleges, schools, local education authorities, learning and skills councils, careers services, training providers and others to work together on an outreach programme in geographical regions and sub-regions. Aimhigher is focused on young people aged 13 to 30. It seeks in particular to reach those young people in school, college or the workplace who have the ability to enter HE but are unlikely to do so without additional support. In particular, these are those from manual backgrounds, as 80 percent of young people from professional backgrounds progress to HE, while only 18 percent of those from unskilled manual backgrounds do so. In addition, those with vocational qualifications are targeted as less than half of all young people who take vocational qualifications at Level 3 go on to enter HE while over 90 percent of those with two or more passes at A-level do so (Action on Access 2005). As a result there are over one million young people in the workforce with Level 3 qualifications who have never entered HE. Certain minority ethnic groups, such as Afro-Caribbean men and Pakistani and Bangladeshi women who remain under-represented in HE and disabled people are also targeted in some projects.

The Aimhigher programme, unlike the TRIO Program, does not specifically target first generation entrants, although each regional and sub-regional partnership is able to define its own target groups within the Aimhigher remit. Broader research in the UK found that in many widening participation interventions target groups are poorly defined (Thomas et al. 2005). The potential implication of lose definitions of target groups is that the actual challenges faced by potential entrants are not identified and tackled head on. The TRIO Program benefits from having clearly defined target groups, which are specified in law. This increases the specificity of targeting and the development of appropriate interventions.

Targeted access programmes like TRIO and Aimhigher are, however, largely informed by the academic model of widening participation, as there is little or no attempt to improve the academic qualifications of these students (for example, in the school system) and there is no attempt to bring about institutional change: Aimhigher focuses on outreach and pre-entry activities, while TRIO does provide some support within higher education, but this is directed towards students rather than institutional change. For

many first generation entrants support and encouragement to change to enter higher education will be insufficient to overcome the long-term consequences of family educational background in relation to their experiences in HE (as demonstrated in Chapter 5).

Incentives to institutions to recruit and retain students
In a number of countries governments give institutions financial incentives to recruit students from under-represented groups. Other countries provide financial incentives for institutions to retain students. For example, in Ireland, finance is provided for specialist access officers who can undertake both an outreach and in-reach function to improve access and student success.

In Australia the Commonwealth Government offers institutions a financial incentive to enrol more students from equity groups, particularly those from low socio-economic backgrounds. The Higher Education Equity Programme (HEEP) provides seed funding for equity initiatives that institutions may wish to implement. This is distributed on the basis of the number of enrolled students in each equity target group and the academic success and retention of those students. Forty percent of institutions' HEEP funding is allocated according to the number of students from low socio-economic backgrounds the institution enrols. Simiarly, in the US federal and state government student aid programmes offer colleges an incentive to provide access to low income students. Since the advent of such incentives low income college participation has risen dramatically.

In England the Higher Education Funding Council (HEFCE), acting on behalf of the government, provides institutions with financial incentives to support student success. The so-called widening participation premium recognizes the differential cost of supporting students from diverse backgrounds, particularly those who do not have traditional educational experiences and who might have additional needs. The money, however, is distributed on the basis of the number of students recruited from low participation neighbourhoods (i.e., geographical area), rather than a criterion such as parental educational background. This money has now been integrated into the institution's core grant from the funding council, which makes monitoring the use of the funding and assessing its benefits more challenging, but it does promote an institution-wide approach.

Providing institutions with financial incentives may give them the inclination and capacity to change, at least in part, what they offer to students. Such a funding strategy therefore can be used to stimulate a transformative approach towards widening participation. In the UK, however, much of the activity appears to have focused on funding further outreach and pre-entry work, rather than institutional development (Thomas et al. 2005). This is particularly true in the more traditional universities, while some of the former polytechnics have adopted more transformative approaches, including curriculum development, pedagogical change and proactive student support. These institutional responses to national strategies indicate the importance of difference in the sector. A more transformative approach could be

fostered in a wider range of institutions by providing greater guidance or restrictions about how the money is spent.

It is important to note that none of these schemes specifically targets first generation entrants. In Australia equity practitioners have sought to persuade the government of the utility of identifying and focusing on first generation entrants as a separate target group (Heagney 2006), but these efforts have not been successful. A specific focus on first generation entrants would alert people to the socio-cultural barriers that these students face in higher education, and draw attention to the need for institutuional change. As discussed in Chapter 6, there is a need for better information, advice and guidance and support to use it; improved learning, teaching and assessment practices; the identification of alternative ways of promoting social integration; greater recognition of the need to undertake paid work, and the incorporation of employment into the learning experience; and a more flexible system that would enable students to negotiate more appropriate learning for themselves.

New universities and new programmes
In other countries seemingly more radical approaches have been utilized by governments to widen participation: namely the development of new qualifications, and even new institutions, to meet the needs of students from under-represented groups. For example, in the UK two year foundation degrees have been conceptualized as an important plank in the national approach to widening participation (DfES 2003b), while in Sweden a significant widening participation strategy has been the creation of new state funded institutions in areas of low participation.

Foundation degrees are two year work-based programmes intended to be developed by partnerships between higher education institutions and employers, which either result in a final qualification at a level lower than an undergraduate degree, or they can be used as a stepping stone towards a degree. This approach is clearly within the utilitarian access discourse, as the main argument initially used to develop foundation degrees was the lack of employees with intermediate qualifications, which was linked to labour market needs and international comparisons. This begs the question, however, as to why these programmes are, or should be, more attractive to non-traditional students? Low income students may find them more economically viable, while first generation entrants may find their explicit link with employment opportunities reassuring. But as foundation degrees are vocational in their focus and associated with lower labour market outcomes (in other words, at intermediate rather than graduate level) it is not clear that these qualifications do offer the best returns (developmentally or financially) to students. Alternatively, if they are to act as a 'stepping stone' to an honours degree programme, then progression routes must be developed and assured.

Irish research notes the invisibility of universities in working class areas (Lynch and Riordan 1998). In Sweden, an interesting strategy has been to

establish new universities located in areas of deprivation, which specifically target students from low socio-economic groups. In the late 1990s a new university was established in Södertörn in the south of Stockholm and Malmö *högskola* was established in the centre of Malmö, both with a specific mission to recruit under-represented groups taking both ethnicity and socio-economic status into account. National data for all universities in Sweden shows that while students from lower socio-economic groups are still under-represented at Södertörn and Malmö compared to their population share, there are considerably more students from these groups participating in higher education than at other universities. Thus, the establishment of new institutions has contributed to an improved national situation too. Arguably, institutions set up with a specific mission should be better at not only attracting these students, but also at retaining them. This approach to widening participation is likely to be informed, at least to some extent, by the transformative model of widening participation, as it is designed to meet the needs of new student cohorts – such as to be near to where they live and provide courses of interest and relevance to them. Such developments may be informed by the needs of the economy too – for example, a shortage of professionals in certain geographical areas. This approach therefore is likely to draw from both the transformative and utilitarian discourses of widening participation.

Targeted strategies are essential if governments are to work towards improving the access and success of students from under-represented groups, and there are a range of types of policy that can be adopted. These, however, can be informed by different principles and support academic, utilitarian or transformative approaches to widening participation. Greater awareness of the different approaches to widening participation might enable governments to either devise strategies that best meet their aspirations, or encourage them to be more prescriptive with regards to how policy is interpreted and implemented by institutions. At present specific targeting at first generation entrants is rare internationally and therefore, arguably, the process fails to pinpoint those who are most in need of support.

Data collection, evaluation and benchmarking

The international study utilized existing national data about students from under-represented groups in higher education. It became apparent that not only do countries collect data differently, and so comparisons are difficult, but also they do not all choose to collect data about the same under-represented groups. Thus, a prerequisite for data collection in relation to a specific sector of society is government-led targeting. A fundamental difference emerges between whether the data is collected directly from students (and their parents) for higher education purposes, or whether existing national data sources are harnessed to provide the information required. The latter is believed to be more reliable and less intrusive, but it relies on

robust and interconnected data sources. In the UK for example, there is no such database which is related to participation in education, but rather information is generated at each stage (for example, at application by the Universities and Colleges Admission Service, and in higher education by institutions). Thus widening participation initiatives in the UK experience a range of data difficulties when trying to assess the impact of their interventions (Thomas et al. 2005). A data set linking school achievement, higher education applications and progression would help overcome this problem, and could be linked to other data sets such as employment (national insurance number) or health (national health service number) to improve the reliability of the data and avoid additional collection. A further distinction can be drawn about whether qualitative as well as quantitative data is collected, as the former can be used to understand patterns shown up by the latter, and help to bring about change.

Data collection itself is a neutral process, but using data, for example to evaluate progress and to compare institutions or regions includes a value judgement. Thus data collection alone will not support students from underrepresented groups to access and succeed in higher education, but this information can be used more or less constructively to further these ends. The international analysis identified approaches to collecting and using information and data that can either inform good practice or drive institutional change.

Collecting good practice
A number of national governments have supported the collection and analysis of approaches to widening participation, with the aim of informing and stimulating further work across the sector. For example in Ireland there have been a number of publications seeking to inform the Irish higher education sector about access issues. Perhaps the most ambitious of these is the study by Skilbeck and Connell (2000) which took an international approach to exploring widening participation policy and practice, and relating it to the Irish context. Similarly, in 1999, 2000 and 2003 the Agency of Higher Education in Sweden collected data from all universities on how they had worked to widen social and ethnic participation in higher education. The result is published in an anthology from the agency. In England, the Higher Education Funding Council and Action on Access, its widening participation national coordination team, have undertaken a range of publications about widening participation practice in the sector, and in 2005 this was extended through a series of international studies to inform practice. Evaluating examples of practice however is problematic, unless it is informed by an explicit framework of what constitutes good practice. Moreover, as discussed in Chapter 2, the transferability of practice from one national setting to another is highly questionable. This approach to widening participation however can be used to endorse and promote an academic, utilitarian or transformative model of widening participation. Through our international study and in the UK we have been able

to find very little work explicitly addressing the needs of first generation entrants.

Systematic evaluation and benchmarking

It is interesting that it is in the country with the lowest rate of access to HE among the ten studied that a systematic and student centred approach to evaluation is being adopted, paying attention to pedagogy and curriculum in ways rarely seen in the other countries. While Croatia cannot be said to work with a blank canvas (the consequences of the Homeland War are perceived as catastrophic, creating a problem of high unemployment and emigration among young people) they are perhaps not as bogged down by layers of educational practice and history as some other nations. They are thus initiating a national evaluation programme to assess and stimulate the quality of teaching in higher education. The data will enable a deeper insight into the causes of low participation and success and provide guidelines for change. At the same time it will develop a methodology for the self-evaluation of institutions as well as university teachers. This study proposes to first survey students as to the quality of their learning experience. The results will then be compared across institutions. A national protocol will then be developed to evaluate and plan strategies for change. This will include self-evaluation, personal development and ongoing focus groups for tutors. This process will then be repeated in two years (Bezinović 2002). This model of evaluation appears to be putting students at the heart of the process, and has much in common with the recently introduced National Student Survey in the UK, while taking the process much further in terms of developing systematic institutional and tutor critique.

These student centred studies have the potential to inform a transformative model of widening participation, but this will require ongoing support and change at the national level to enable institutions to move from their current *modus operandi* to a new one. The process of institutional change can be encouraged at the national level through a process of benchmarking – comparing institutions against each other. In Ireland this has been attempted more informally via the access officers, whereas in the UK performance indicator tables have been established to compare institutions' actual performance against expected performance, and to facilitate comparison between similar institutions. Benchmarking, however, is not specifically aligned with a particular model of widening participation, rather institutional mission and history is more likely to inform how groups of institutions will strive to improve their relative positions. Thus, in the UK institutions with a mission of academic excellence, as opposed perhaps to student diversity, and a strong track record of selecting rather than recruiting students, are more likely to adopt an academic approach to widening participation, seeking to attract well qualified applicants who might have attended other institutions or not entered HE at all. Other institutions may seek to change their provision to make it more attractive to potential students and to support them to succeed – this may be supported by either

a utilitarian or a transformative approach to widening participation. There are no examples available of a systematic evaluation or student centred approach which specifically focuses on the experiences of first generation entrants in higher education. Our qualitative study (reported in Chapter 6) appears to be an important contribution to understanding first generation entrants experiences, and reinforces the need for institutional and systemic transformation.

Research, training and staff development
Information and research has to be utilized to have an impact on the student experience. In Norway efforts have been made to undertake research and use this to inform training and staff development to support the needs of a more diverse tertiary education sector. For example, in June 2002 a new network for diversity training in Norwegian public services was established. The network is for people working in a broad spectre of key public sectors at national and regional level, including higher education institutions. The diversity training is intended to ensure consistent high quality in public services, equal opportunities, equal obligations and equal rights for minority groups. The purposes of the network are: exchange of knowledge and information; competence development; information of the members' competence and experience; and mutual inspiration. Although the secretariat is run by the Norwegian Directorate of Immigration and the focus is on supporting the needs of minority groups, it offers a model of how information and research about diversity more generally could be employed at a national level to enhance students' experiences. More specifically, the Centre for Development of Competence in the Multicultural School, Oslo University College, Norway (*Senter for kompetanseutvikling i den flerkulturelle skolen* – SEFS) is financed by the Ministry of Education and Research. Its purpose is to support institutional and staff development to meet the needs of a multicultural higher education population. The centre collects information and undertakes research and uses this to inform institutional managers and staff through networks, lectures and briefings.

Alternative admissions procedures

In many countries there are nationally set standards for entering higher education, for example, obtaining a high school certificate is a common requirement. Governments and higher education systems can therefore play a role in widening participation by offering alternative entry routes and influencing the allocation of places to students from under-represented groups. In the international study two key approaches emerged, one relating to improving the opportunities open to qualified applicants from non-traditional groups, and the second concerned recognition of alternative qualifications or experience as relevant to study at HE level. Both of these types of changes require systemic and/or institutional change, rather than

students changing, which therefore helps to address the prevalence of deficit approaches to widening participation.

Improving opportunities for qualified applicants
In many countries students from under-represented groups experience disadvantage when they seek to enter competitive institutions or subjects. For example, a review of research evidence in the UK shows that students from equity groups are more likely to attend a post-1992 institution or a further education college than other, more prestigious, universities (Gorard et al. 2006). Students from lower socio-economic groups are more likely to participate in some discipline areas such as education, and less likely to participate in others, such as medicine (Thomas et al. 2005). Subjects such as law and medicine are, however, much more competitive to enter than some other subject areas. First generation entrants can be particularly disadvantaged when selection is made by interview as they may lack the confidence and breadth of knowledge of students from more privileged backgrounds, and in addition there may be ingrained prejudice against them from admissions staff.

The Netherlands has implemented a system of a 'weighted draw' for certain 'numerous fixes' courses, those where there is a limited number of places and too many applicants. To be entered in the draw students need to achieve a threshold level, which represents sufficient ability to benefit from and succeed in higher education. Beyond this, allocation of places is random. In the Netherlands the system has been recently amended so that the chances of success are higher the higher the grades achieved, and certain students are allocated places automatically without taking part in the draw, however, random selection remains a significant part of the process. In Scotland pioneering work (Osborne and Lumsden 2005) is exploring the utility of psychometric and similar testing of young people to identify those who have suitable personal characteristics for a career in medicine and the health professions. While this work is in the early stages, initial findings show that suitability is evenly distributed across socio-economic groups, and these tests, combined with academic qualifications, could contribute to fairer access to higher education, particularly in competitive areas such as medicine, as well as in selecting the people most suited to being health care professionals. These types of approaches to allocating places in higher education would help prevent the development of institutional and disciplinary hierarchies and ghettos and would certainly contribute to a more utilitarian and less academic approach to widening participation, and may even help to promote some transformation of the system.

Alternative entry routes
Providing first generation entrants and people from lower socio-economic groups with an opportunity to compensate for early disadvantage by entering HE when they are older, which may include offering different entry requirements is a strategy which is deployed by a range of countries.

This second chance is sometimes, as in the UK, facilitated by alternative entry qualifications obtained via further education or adult education. But in Sweden and Norway the second chance route is based more on work experience than the attainment of academic qualifications. In Sweden all those who are 25 or older and have four years gainful employment are eligible for entry into higher education. Norway has a lower age limit of 23 but requires five years of employment and the ability to meet certain academic core subject requirements. It is interesting that in this capacity 'work' includes being a primary caregiver, which is clearly a beneficial step towards gender equality. Ireland appears to have created particularly flexible pathways from further education to higher education involving part-time study and combinations of work and study which are tailored to suit the learning development and lifestyle of the individual.

The provision of alternative entry routes offers students who did not progress to higher education when they were younger the opportunity to participate later in life. Requiring students to obtain comparable academic qualifications can be seen to fit within the academic discourse of widening participation, while a work experience route takes much more account of student diversity, and thus appears more transformative (assuming students entering via this route are able to access all discipline areas and not just vocational programmes, when it would be more appropriate to categorize the approach as utilitarian). Widespread availability of alternative entry routes, as in Norway and Sweden, would offer first generation entrants greater flexibility, and if they did not enter HE as young students, they would have opportunities more readily available at a later date.

Alternative delivery

In a number of countries that participated in our study widening participation objectives have been furthered through the introduction of alternative ways of delivering higher education. This has included the establishment of new institutions and more flexible delivery modes.

New institutions

Geography can have a significant impact on the participation of students from some under-represented groups. Recent research in the UK found that many first generation entrants were unwilling or unable to move away from home to study in higher education, and thus preferred local provision, even if the course was not their first choice (Quinn et al. 2005; see also UCAS 2002). The preference for local provision may reflect perceived and actual geographical distance, as well and cultural distance (Wynn-Williams et al. 1999). A small-scale study in the UK found that a major reason for not continuing with study was distance to the nearest college, and for the ethnic minority women involved in the study it was the psychological distance from family responsibilities rather than the actual travel involved that was

problematic (Hramiak 2001). As noted above, to overcome distance barriers, the Swedish parliament established higher education institutions in a number of new locations and also allocated more study places to new universities in the 1990s. By these means, opportunities to study in Swedish higher education have been more evenly spread across the country and this has tended to equalize transition rates to HE. This has been complemented by the provision of more distance learning education in regional centres (Thomas 2001). As discussed above, the provision of new institutions is likely to be informed, at least to some extent, by the transformative model of widening participation as well as local labour market needs.

Distance learning
Distance education has been posited as one route to widen participation among under-represented groups in many countries (Osborne 2003), both in nations with well developed tertiary education and those where tertiary education is in a more emergent state. In Croatia, for example, it is seen as a key aspect of their growing national strategy and the Faculty of Organization and Informatics in Varaždin (University of Zargreb) has become a Referral Centre for the Application of E-learning Projects. In the UK Learndirect centres have been established to facilitate on-line access to a wide range of learning opportunities. Dhillon's (2004) research with students studying at Learndirect centres found that proximity to home and convenience for travel were strong factors influencing their participation in this type of learning. This suggests that distance learning can overcome some of the limitations of access, but there is little evidence to support the claim that it is attracting new learners to HE (rather than ones who would have gone to higher education anyway) (Gorard et al. 2006). Furthermore, retention on distance learning programmes tends to be lower than for other courses (Simpson 2003), suggesting that learning at a distance and/or using technology brings its own challenges, especially in relation to widening participation (Noble 2004). E-learning and distance learning can be used to support any of the widening participation discourses, as it depends on the curriculum rather than mode of delivery. It may, however, be particularly challenging for first generation entrants to develop appropriate learning attitudes and practices with little prior knowledge to guide them if they are working at a distance from the institution and other learners (see Postle et al. 2000).

Institutional approaches to supporting first generation entrants

This section of the chapter explores ways in which particular higher education institutions have responded to the challenge of extending access to first generation entrants and supporting them to be successful within higher education. Like the previous section it draws largely from our international

study (Thomas and Quinn 2003a). Given the scale and nature of the study (as discussed in Chapter 2), the examples discussed here are illustrative rather than exhaustive. It is noticeable that there are only limited examples of interventions explicitly targeted at first generation entrants (15 percent in Thomas et al. 2005), and further research has found that institutions may mention first generation entrants, but they have not developed programmes specifically targeted at them. Research, however, suggests that to have the greatest positive effect, interventions should explicitly and accurately target groups, rather than use a scatter-gun effect (Woodrow 1998). An analysis of institutional approaches to targeting a range of under-represented groups identified ways in which institutions could develop specific interventions for first generation entrants. The key responses have been categorized into pre-entry work, supporting students within the institution and data collection and institutional research. These approaches are now discussed and considered in relation to widening participation discourses.

Pre-entry work

Many institutions have examples of pre-entry work designed to enable people to attend higher education. It is noticeable from the international study and from research in the UK (Gorard et al. 2006) that the majority of these interventions are with young people, often in a school setting. This may reflect both national and institutional policy priorities and convenience. Some pre-entry work focuses almost exclusively on the provision of information and raising awareness of higher education opportunities, while other activities include efforts to improve academic achievement prior to entry, and strategies to equip students for the transition into higher education learning. The former falls within the academic access approach, while other approaches are utilitarian; there is little attempt to transform the schooling experience. The main approaches used are: student mentors, ambassadors and role models delivering activities in schools, campus visits and taster sessions and summer schools, usually with a residential element.

Some examples of pre-entry work and given in the boxes below.

Wise Up is a six day summer school based at the *University of Manchester.* It targets lower socio-economic groups and first generation entrants from secondary schools in the region. Through a mixture of academic, careers and skills based sessions, balanced with social activities it gives the Year 11 students an idea of what university life would be like. The students work with the university's academic staff attending curriculum sessions. They are supervised and supported by the Widening Participation team and existing students throughout the week. Students work on a research project for the six days, improving their research,

communication, teambuilding and presentation skills. The week cul-
minates in a graduation ceremony to which friends and family are
invited.

Waterford Institute of Technology in Ireland runs a summer school specifically for mature entrants. Many of these students have not completed
their school and may feel less well prepared for study than their
younger peers. The aim of the summer school is to improve academic
preparation, and to build the confidence of the learners, many of
whom are first generation entrants.

The *University of South Australia* has established an equity initiative
called USANET (University of South Australia Networking; see
www.unisa. edu.au). The aim of the scheme is to provide greater access,
participation, and success in higher education for students who have
been educationally disadvantaged by either economic circumstances or
distance. The focus of the scheme is to encourage a wider group of
students to consider university as a realistic option and to support them
during their studies. The three components of the USANET scheme are:

- *Outreach*: Targeting approved secondary schools and TAFE institutions.
- *Support*: Providing programmes of support for students who enrol
  through the scheme.
- *Access*: Aiming to increase enrolments into the university and to
  provide assistance to students enrolled in approved USANET targeted secondary schools. There are two streams of these schools:
  schools with a high proportion of enrolments from low income
  backgrounds, and schools in rural and isolated areas.

The High Skies student tutoring scheme is led by the *University of the
West of England (UWE) in collaboration with the University of Bristol.* It targets
school students from lower socio-economic groups, low participation
neighbourhoods, first generation entrants and low income groups.
Undergraduates are selected and recruited to take part in the scheme
according to key criteria such as family/school background, subject
areas offered, timetable constraints and suitability for the student
tutoring role. Training is provided to the undergraduates, to enable
them to deliver a range of activities, including school visits, telephone
and email support, meetings with school and university staff, etc.

Undergraduates work across a range of year groups under the direction of a classroom teacher.

The *SEUR project in Canada* (*Sensibilisation aux Études Universitaires et à la Recherche*; programme to promote university studies and research; see http://www.seur.qc.ca/index.html) gives high school students from target groups the opportunity to meet with the university's research teams during the school year, with visits to research laboratories for small groups of school pupils, and mentoring by researchers for science research projects that are of interest to the high school students, and this includes making both expertise and the laboratory facilities available to the students.

The Student Shadowing Day at *De Montfort University* aims to give young people the opportunity to experience a day in the life of an undergraduate student. The young people involved are first generation entrants, from low income groups, low participation neighbourhoods, lower socio-economic groups or working class backgrounds. Undergraduates work with a small number of Year 11 pupils who have an interest in a particular field of study, taking them to their course lectures and seminars, showing them around the university campus including halls of residence, and discussing issues such as student finance, student welfare services and life at university.

The *Access to Birmingham Admissions Scheme* targets applicants from local state schools who are first generation into higher education. Schools provide an additional reference for the admissions tutor to consider and applicants prepare a supplementary form. If accepted onto the scheme, applicants receive a slightly lower offer (typically one or two grades below standard offer) and have to successfully complete the Foundations of Learning module before final acceptance. In addition, applicants are required to make Birmingham their first choice institution.

Research in the UK (Thomas et al. 2005) has found that pre-entry work has developed since a similar earlier study (Woodrow 1998). Institutions are starting to work with younger children (e.g., in primary school) and through programmes of activities stretching throughout their school career, thus recognizing the need for early and sustained intervention (see also Morris et al. 2005). Furthermore, there is evidence of greater engagement of

parents. Indeed, in an English study, Pennell et al. (2005) found that 70 percent of HEIs responding to their survey had parent focused activities. Accurately targeting pupils, however, remains a difficulty. Most interventions use a broad notion of 'lower socio-economic status' (SES) rather than explicitly identifying groups based on income, occupation, geography or parental education. The majority of interventions focus on specific schools rather than individual children as a proxy for more specific information. For example, the school's HE participation rate may be used, or the proportion of pupils attaining five GSCEs or more. While this keeps the process simple and does not involve obtaining information about individual circumstances, it does not ensure that those young people who have the most to gain from interventions are the most likely to benefit from them. When pupils from within a particular school are selected, the majority of interventions leave the selection process to the schools or colleges. Selection procedures tend to be imprecise and schools use their own strategies of selection which may meet their own needs (Thomas and Slack 1999). The use of 'champion teachers' who understand, support and promote widening access activities has been used by some initiatives, for example the University of Bangor's Talent Opportunities Programme.

An analysis of research evidence related to school-based interventions suggests that to have the greatest positive effect on young people:

- Targeting has to be explicit and overseen by the intervention rather than the school, otherwise the intended beneficiaries may be excluded and others included (Woodrow 1998; Thomas and Slack 2000). Some evidence suggests that some pupils are better able to take advantage of activities, and without careful targeting the gap between groups of pupils may increase (Thomas and Slack 1999);
- Activities have to be of interest and relevant to the young people (Thomas and Slack 1999);
- Activities need to be interactive and engaging (Thomas and Slack 2000; Greater Merseyside Aimhigher 2003). Greater Merseyside Aimhigher (2003) found that practical, hands-on activities, project/problem-based activities, team work in small groups with an undergraduate facilitator were more engaging in the view of staff and pupils;
- School cultures and activities have to reinforce widening participation interventions (Thomas and Slack 2000; Morris et al. 2005); and
- Parents need to be involved in activities: in Year 9, parents (Thomas and Slack 2000), and in particular mothers (McLinden 2003), were considered the main influence on young people's decision making.

Supporting students within the institution

Enabling and supporting students to enter higher education is only part of the challenge, as Chapter 6 has highlighted. An equally important issue is

supporting those students to succeed. The academic approach to access does not see this issue as being of particular concern, as the emphasis is on entry for able students. A utilitarian approach views student retention and completion as a high priority to enable contribution to society and the economy, while a transformative approach perceives the experience within HE as important. The utilitarian approach tends to focus on supporting students to succeed, while the transformative approach is more dialogical, requiring both institutional and student development and mutually beneficial returns.

In the UK much of the work to support students to succeed has taken place in the early stages through transition and induction programmes. For example, the University of Central Lancashire's Flying Start programme was originally established to address the issue that students with vocational rather than academic qualifications – GNVQs as opposed to A-levels and who were predominantly from low socio-economic groups and first generation entrants – were not succeeding academically and dropping out at a much higher rate than other entrants. The summer school involved all GNVQ students, who had accepted a place at the university, in various academic, social, networking and activities to demystify university procedures and HE study activities. Careful tracking of these students revealed that retention rates are much higher for them than for students as a whole and the intervention has since been extended to other targeted groups of entrants. This is a good example of a utilitarian approach to supporting students, and some institutional transformation has occurred as a result of learning from the students involved in the pre-entry summer school.

Being at university is a social and cultural experience as well as an opportunity to learn. However, this culture may be an alien one for the students from these target groups and their families and this alienation can be exacerbated by curriculum and teaching strategies which do not take into account the diversity of the student body. A number of studies (see, for example, Lynch and O'Riordan 1998 writing in an Irish context; and Thomas 2002 writing in an English context) have emphasized the importance of addressing social and cultural barriers faced by the target groups. Creating a sense of 'belonging' partly derives from taking part in other activities. Volunteering and mutual help offer a way for students to engage with their institution and to meet other students, which in turn has academic as well as social benefits. Canadian research (Grayson 1995) found that greater involvement in university activities by traditional students contributes to their higher Grade Point Average. Blasko et al. (2003) found that participation in extra curricular activities improved students' opportunities in the graduate labour market. Chester College encourages all students, and particularly those who struggle with the transition to higher education, to become involved in volunteering. In one initiative, the volunteers provide personal support to other students from similar backgrounds, even from the same deprived residential area, countering homesickness and insecurity. In turn this helps to produce feelings of belonging, and thus promotes the retention and success of both volunteers and students using the support services.

In Australia and Ireland mature students are facilitated to develop their own support networks via mature student clubs or cooperatives. For example, the Centre for Helping Access, Retention and Teaching (CHART) at Waterford Institute of Technology, Ireland, has supported the development of a mature students' club and a parents' club. These may be perceived as utilitarian approaches to student support, but they do entail some aspects of transformation, as the institutions recognize the support that one student can offer another. There is clearly scope for mutual support to be developed for first generation entrants, who face many similar challenges in their higher education experience.

A key area for support is in relation to academic development. According to Warren (2002) academic interventions can be separate, semi-integrated or integrated. A separate approach implies that the intervention of support is offered in addition to mainstream teaching, for example supplementary instruction or skills modules. These initiatives articulate with the utilitarian approach to widening participation. A semi-integrated approach includes interventions which are closely aligned to curriculum and which are developmental rather than 'remedial' in character; these therefore fall into the utilitarian and transformative approaches. Integrated approaches make the development central to the learning experience within the discipline context, and are most likely to be found within a transformative environment. To facilitate a more integrated approach the University of Monash, Australia, has a faculty level programme which embeds the student in their new academic discipline, and this is compulsory for the validation of all new academic programmes. In Ireland, special funding from the government, through the Higher Education Authority, has enabled a number of institutions to integrate study skills into the curriculum (Thornhill 2002).

Data collection and institutional research

Yorke and Thomas (2003) found that one aspect of success in relation to retaining students from lower socio-economic groups included institutional data collection and research, and the utilization of this information. Data collection and research is essential for the transformation of higher education institutions. In Canada the Consortium on Student Success in Higher Education at the University of Quebec draws on research from the past 20 years on the student pathway, and uses this information to improve the student experience. This initiative began as institutional research at the University of Quebec, but has received recognition and financial support from the Minister of Education to form a consortium consisting of professors and researchers from universities and colleges all over Quebec with the aim of collecting, analysing and disseminating research and information about students' success in HE and the effectiveness of intervention strategies. The consortium is able to draw from this corpus of information in order to create a real bank of knowledge on student success; encourage the best use of the

information within the institutional context; support the revision of the success strategies; and to promote measures which have proven successful.

Institutional research at The Open University (OU) in the UK has been used to demonstrate the need to re-introduce a form of personal support for students who are at risk of early withdrawal from higher education (Simpson 2006). Staff undertook an experiment involving 3000 students who were identified as being particularly vulnerable to drop out by a statistical analysis of their entry characteristics. Half were proactively phoned before their courses started by a 'study adviser', while the others were not contacted and thus acted as a control group. The experiment was repeated in three successive years. On average the experimental group had a retention rate around 5 percent higher than the control group. Simpson suggests the following reasons why such a simple phone call could have had such an effect:

- Student dropout in the OU is heavily front-loaded. About 15 percent of students drop out before courses start and another 30 percent in the period before submitting the first assignment. They therefore have little contact with their tutor and any teaching activity. Thus to have much effect on retention it is likely that an activity needs to be focused before or at the start of the courses.
- There is no personal proactive contact from the university before courses start. Potential students are encouraged to enrol with the university on the Web and are therefore unlikely to have any personal contact with the university before course materials arrive. Thus a personal interactive contact stands out and may consequently have a marked result.
- The style of the contact was an individually focused activity aimed at enhancing the student's motivation rather than on identifying weaknesses. It is therefore reassuring and confidence building, rather than being challenging.

Despite the potential of institutional data and research to improve access to higher education and students experience within HE, there is evidence from the UK that many institutions do not use these resources to anywhere like their full potential. Layer et al. (2002) found that institutions do not disaggregate institutional data to explore which students are leaving higher education early, and Thomas et al. (2005) found that there is a weak link between academic educational and social research departments and widening participation interventions.

Conclusions

This chapter has discussed the alternative approaches to widening participation from both theoretical and practical perspectives. This has revealed that there is very little explicit recognition of the impact of parental education. Implicitly, the academic discourse of widening access recognizes some aspects of first generation entry, namely that these students may lack the

aspiration to enter higher education that is instilled in families with a tradition of participation in HE. However, it neglects the complexities of first generation entry acknowledged in Chapter 4 and the broader influences of parental education discussed in Chapter 5: in particular the way parental education influences and interacts with other aspects of child development, such as school attended and academic achievements, and parental employment and family income. Thus, the academic approach to widening participation focuses predominantly on access to HE for young people who have demonstrated that they have the academic ability to enter into selective institutions. An important omission from the academic access discourse is the recognition of the impact of parental education and family background on the experience of students within higher education, and how this affects their ability to thrive and succeed in HE (as discussed in Chapter 6).

The utilitarian approach to widening participation takes account of a wider range of barriers to access to higher education, and provides greater support for student success. However, it is more ambiguous as to the weight given to the different types of capital that students have access to. The utilitarian approach can, for example, focus on students' financial capital, and this can be used to justify shorter, cheaper vocational qualifications that simultaneously meet the needs of the economy. Utilitarian approaches to supporting student success tend to try to compensate for perceived gaps in students' stocks of capital, rather than seeking to change national and institutional systems that require students to have access to certain types of economic, social and cultural capital. Again, this support can focus on financial capital, for example, through the provision of discretionary bursaries; on cultural capital, for example, by providing additional opportunities for academic skills development; or on social capital, for example, through pre-entry activities that provide students with additional information about higher education and enable them to meet peers.

The transformative approach to widening participation recognizes the ways in which higher education privileges and prioritizes the values and *modus operandi* of middle class students over students from under-represented and non-traditional backgrounds. Thus, the objective of transformative interventions is to change national and institutional practices to enable them to be informed by a wider range of expectations, values and experiences. The emphasis therefore is not just on access to higher education, but on delivering an HE experience which is of relevance to all students, and which enables them to succeed.

An analysis of practical ways in which national HE systems and higher education institutions are promoting the widening of participation illustrates that explicit recognition of first generation entry does not happen frequently. When first generation entrants are identified as a target group, it is usually in a list, including low income and low socio-economic groups. Thus, the specific and direct influences of parental background are not taken into consideration when interventions are planned and implemented, even though the analysis in this book demonstrates their importance.

The influence of parental education is far reaching and pervasive – influencing school attended, academic success, progression to HE and experience within higher education, thus some students have educational pathways or trajectories that need disrupting and/or accommodating. Skilbeck and Connell (2000) highlight the fact that HE cannot be seen in isolation from other factors which produce inequality. Their notion of an educational equity chain is a useful one providing a framework of objectives describing how opportunity can be extended from early childhood learning to postgraduate study and career progression. However, this image of a chain also highlights how it can be broken and fragmented, making progression impossible. Building transitions which effectively take into account the barriers faced by these target groups is vital: this includes familiarization with the institution pre-entry; effective transition and induction processes; building systems of mentoring and peer support; integrated curriculum support; and opportunities for social networking and integration.

There is comparatively little emphasis on intervention in the early years – even though this may be an effective way of changing participation patterns (Parker and Courtney 1998). There is some evidence, however, that the impact of interventions is at best modest, as the influence of the family, home and community is likely to be much more powerful (Gorard et al. 2006). The alternative approach is to review the purpose of higher education and what it currently offers, and to see how this relates to the needs of first generation entrants. This may include being available locally on a daily rather than a residential basis, learning in different ways and studying different subject areas. Currently, however, there is a vocational/academic divide which may reinforce difference, and which does not necessarily correspond to the preferences and aptitudes of students from under-represented groups (Jones 2006).

Our study of first generation entrants (Quinn et al. 2005) indicates that the transformation needs to be far more radical. They can be seen as the real lifelong learners seeking a flexible higher education system which allows for free movements across subjects and institutions, from full-time to part-time mode and which can accommodate breaks in study. Such a system would build on informal learning within families and communities rather than positioning the latter simply as places to escape from. Flexibility and fluidity would be regarded as healthy and not aberrant. The challenge for HE policy makers is to catch up with this vision and these learners.

8
The implications of first generation entry for redefining widening participation

Our international analysis of policy, practice, data and research indicated that parental education and first generation entry are important variables in relation to students' experiences of higher education, but which are often either neglected, or subsumed within a catchall concept of socio-economic status (Thomas and Quinn 2003a). In this book we have been able to explore the importance of these issues further. We believe that both our international analysis and our UK study have added to the store of knowledge on first generation entry and that this book has enabled us to focus on the issues that they generate. This has been accomplished by a synthesis and analysis of research and grey literature from ten countries; by analysis of theoretical literature on the family; and by a qualitative analysis of in depth data of first generation entrants in the UK.

One of the problems we have faced in writing a book on this subject is that there is so little targeted information about first generation entry as such. As we have shown, an international perspective reveals the particular importance of parental education to ongoing patterns of progression and success in HE, and yet it is almost always subsumed into more general debates about socio-economic status which focus on income, employment or geography. One response to this problem has been to draw on socio-cultural literature on the family and this has enabled us to take a fresh look at the issue. Understanding first generation entry as a process of reciprocity within families, families which are themselves increasingly perceived in terms of fluid relationships rather than as rigid structures, enables us to understand how complex and ambivalent first generation entry is.

First generation entry is dominantly discursively framed as taking the family to a new and better position in society and in many respects our UK study showed that families themselves endorsed this view. However, they did not see university education as vital to a fulfilled and happy life, and both parents and children chose family harmony over miserably staying at university. Moreover, HE was seen as an opportunity to do something useful rather than as a chance to be a different person. It was framed and constrained by the

family in direct and indirect ways. Students had little choice over whether to attend local universities and often lived at home because of the financial problems faced by the family. Parents were usually in low paid and semi-skilled jobs, itself a direct consequence of their lack of opportunities for university study. Parents made every effort to support them throughout their study, but their own lack of experience of university education meant they were unable to give informed advice about courses and institutions, or to help their children to negotiate the system. This doubtless made the experience more difficult for these students. However, the desire of both parents and students to be flexible in relation to studying for a degree, even though they were often positioned as 'stuck' by a lack of local opportunities and the negative attitudes of others such as careers officers, was significant and needs emphasizing.

Our UK study demonstrates that qualitatively first generation entry has a significant impact on university study. What are the implications of this for policy? As we have seen in the ten nations of our international study, first generation entrants are only a target group in a small number of countries. We believe the evidence is strong that first generation entrants should be explicitly targeted within widening participation policy and that this is the best way of ensuring those who most need support will receive it. We are not arguing that minority ethnic groups, for example, or those with disabilities, should not also be targeted, but these loose categories inevitably contain within them families where educational capital is high. By targeting parental education those who experience double disadvantage can be reached directly.

As we have shown in Chapter 3, it is very difficult to disaggregate parental education from socio-economic status, but this does not mean they are entirely the same. If it were a choice between targeting parental education or socio-economic status, we would argue that parental education should be used, as it is the most sensitive indicator of inequality and it is information that is more straightforward to gather. Focusing on first generation entry can help surmount some of the problems inherent in employment definitions of socio-economic status, which are increasingly seen as rather blunt instruments which do not readily respond to social and cultural change or reflect other types of informal labour. However, we would endorse the approach recommended in Canada where both factors are targeted simultaneously. Ultimately we argue that rather than being placed on the periphery or disregarded altogether, parental education should be the key focus for our efforts regarding widening participation.

What should those efforts be? Our analysis indicates that raising the aspirations of parents and families is not the issue. Parents want their children to have access to university opportunities that will sustain family harmony and promote family prosperity. When the available opportunities seem to offer neither of those things, they are put aside without absolute qualms. This is not proof that these families lack values, rather that these values are different from those that are understood to drive higher education systems. This

suggests that rather than trying to fit the family to the university, the university should be thinking more about responding to the needs of the family. It necessitates the transformative approach to HE that we have discussed in Chapter 7. This means that assumptions cannot be made that students and families will possess insider knowledge of HE, and systems, procedures and essential curriculum information should be made both transparent and understandable. On a deeper level it means that a more flexible higher education needs to be developed, and one that recognizes and takes account of different forms of knowledge.

Where next? We see this book as opening up the issue of first generation entry to further investigation and debate. For ourselves, we seek to deepen our understanding of how policy makers are currently engaging with this issue internationally and how institutions are developing responses that target and support first generation entrants. The dynamic impacts of first generation entry on families and the ways in which it can draw parents themselves back into formal learning are also of particular interest to us, in the context of *life-wide* and lifelong learning. The current divide exhibited in educational research and practice, between widening participation activities and community-based informal learning, is a false and unhelpful one. Making first generation entry the locus of investigation is one way in which theoretical and practical bridges can be built. We firmly believe that progress can only be made by change at both the conceptual and material level: rethinking and remaking the widening of participation to fully meet the needs of first generation entrants.

References

Abramson, M. and Jones, P. (2004). Empowering Under-represented Students to Succeed in Higher Education, in D. Saunders, K. Brosnan, M. Walker et al. (eds) *Learning Transformations: Changing Learners, Organisations and Communities.* London: Forum for the Advancement of Continuing Education.

Action on Access (2005) Progression to higher education from vocational, work-based and work-related learning. *Making a Difference: The Impact of Aimhigher.* London: Action on Access.

Action Group on Access (2001) *Report of the Action Group on Access to Third Level Education.* Dublin: Stationery Office.

Agbo, S. (2000) Heterogeneity of the student body and the meaning of 'non-traditional' in US higher education, in H. Schuetze and M. Slowey (eds) *Higher Education and Lifelong Learning: International perspectives on change.* London: Routledge/Falmer.

Aitken, D., Skuja, E. and Schapper, C. (2004) Do Scholarships Help? Preliminary Results of a Case Study of Students in Scholarship Programmes at Monash University, 1997–2001, *Widening Participation and Lifelong Learning,* 6(1).

Albrow, M. and E. King (eds) (1990) *Globalization, Knowledge and Society.* London: Sage/ISA.

Allen, L., Thomas, L., Solomon, L. and Storan, J. (2005) *Indebted to Learning: Balancing Fees, Aid and Access in US Higher Education.* Bradford: Action on Access.

ACE (American Council on Education) (2002) *Access and Persistence: Findings from 10 Years of Longitudinal Research on Students.* Washington, DC: ACE.

Archer, L. and Yamashita, H. (2003) 'Knowing their limits'? Identities, inequalities and inner city school leavers' post-16 aspirations, *Journal of Education Policy,* 18(1): 53–69.

Archer, L., Hutchings, M. and Ross, A. (2003) *Higher Education and Social Class.* London: Routledge Falmer.

Atkinson, E. (2000) In defence of ideas, or why 'what works' is not enough, *British Journal of Sociology of Education,* 21(3): 317–30.

Ball, C. (1989) *Widening Access to Higher Education.* London: RSA.

Ball, S. J. (1990) *Politics and Policy Making in Education.* London: Routledge.

Bamber, J. and Tett, L. (2000) Transforming the learning experiences of

non-traditional students: A perspective from higher education, *Studies in Continuing Education*, 22(1): 57–75.

Bamber, J. and Tett, L. (2001) 'Ensuring integrative learning experiences for non-traditional students', *Widening Participation and Lifelong Learning*, 3(1): 8–16

Bargh, C. Scott, P. and Smith, D. (1994) *Access and Consolidation: The Impact of Reduced Student Intakes on Opportunities for* Non-standard Applicants. Leeds: University of Leeds Centre for Policy Studies in Education.

Beck, U. and Beck-Gernsheim, E. (2002) *Individualization*. London: Sage.

Berg, van den M. N. (2002) *Studeren? (G)een punt! Een kwantitatieve studie naar de studievoortgang in het Nederlandse wetenschappelijk onderwijs in de periode 1996–2000*. Amsterdam: Thela Thesis.

Bezinović, P. (2002) *The Quality of Studies from the Students' Perspective: Guidelines for Changes (Rijeka, Zagreb, Osijek, Split)*. Zagreb: Centre for Educational Research and Development at the Institute for Social Research.

Biggart, A., Deacon, K., Dobbie, F. et al. (2004) *Findings from the Scottish School Leavers Survey: 17 in 2003*. Available at http://www.scotland.gov.uk/library5/education/edrf4–00.asp

Blackmore, C. and Ison, R. (1998) Boundaries for thinking and action, in A. Thomas, J. Chataway and M. Wuyts (eds) *Finding Out Fast: Investigative Skills for Policy and Development*. London: Sage Publications.

Bland, D. (2001) Empowering the disadvantaged: how students from non-traditional backgrounds become leaders in student politics, in E. Thomas, M. Cooper and J. Quinn (eds) *Access to Higher Education: The Unfinished Business*. Stoke-on-Trent: Trentham Books.

Blasko, Z. et al. (2003) *Access to What: Analysis of Factors Determining Graduate Employability*. London: Centre for Higher Education Research.

Blicharski, J. (1998) Disadvantaged youngsters: raising awareness, aspiration and access through a summer school, in J. Preece, C. Weatherald and M. Woodrow (eds) *Beyond the Boundaries: Exploring the Potential of Widening Provision in Higher Education*. Leicester: NIACE.

Blicharski, J. (2000) Tracking students' progression: Learning their Lessons, *Widening Participation and Lifelong Learning*, 2(3): 32–7.

Bonin, S. (2004) Working class student drop out trends in Canada. Paper presented at International perspectives on working class students withdrawal colloquium, Staffordshire University, 28 June.

Bourdieu, P. ([1986] 1997) The forms of capital, in A.H. Halsey, H. Lauder, P. Brown and A.S. Wells (eds) *Education, Culture, Economy, Society*. Oxford: Oxford University Press.

Bourdieu, P. and Passeron, J.C. (1977) *Reproduction in Education, Society and Culture*. London: Sage.

Bowl, M. (2001) Experiencing the barriers: non-traditional students entering higher education, *Research Papers in Education*, 16(2): 141–60.

Bron, A. and Agélii, K. (2000) Non-traditional students in higher education in Sweden: from recurrent education to lifelong learning, in H. Schuetze and M. Slowey (eds) *Higher Education and Lifelong Learning. International Perspectives on Change*. London: Routledge/Falmer.

Brooks, R. (2003) Young people's higher education choices: the role of family and friends, *British Journal of Sociology of Education*, 24(3): 283–97.

Brooks, R. (2004) My mum would be pleased as Punch if I went, but my dad is more

particular about it: paternal involvement in young people's higher education choices, *British Educational Research Journal*, 30(4): 496–514.

Brown, P. and Hesketh, A.J. (2003) *The Social Construction of Graduate Employability*. ESRC research report available at http://www.regard.ac.uk/research_findings/ R000239101/report.pdf

Callender, C. (2003) *Attitudes to Debt: School Leavers and Further Education Students' Attitudes to Debt and their Impact on Participation in Higher Education*. London: Universities UK.

Carpenter, A. (2003) *Irish National Report*. Available at: http://www.staffs.ac.uk/ access-studies

Castles, J. (2004) Persistence and the adult learner: factors affecting persistence in Open University students, *Active Learning in HE*, 5(2): 166–79.

Chapman, B. and Ryan, C. (2002) Income contingent financing of student higher education charges: assessing the Australian innovation, *Welsh Journal of Education*, 11: 64–81.

Chataway and Wuyts, M. (eds) (1998) *Finding Out Fast: Investigative Skills for Policy and Development*. London: Sage.

Chenard, P. and Bonin, S. (2003) *Canadian National Report*. Available at: www.staffs.ac.uk/access-studies

Choy, S. (2002) *Access and Persistence: Findings from Ten Years of Longitudinal Research on Students*. Washington, DC: American Council of Education, Center for Policy Analysis.

Clancy, P. (2001) *College Entry in Focus: A Fourth National Survey of Access to Higher Education*. Dublin: Higher Education Authority. Available at: www.hea.ie

Coates, G. and Adnett, N. (2003) Encouraging cream skimming and dreg-siphoning? Increasing competition between English HEIs, *British Journal of Widening Participation and Lifelong Learning*, 2(3): 14–22.

Coleman, J. S. (1990) *Foundations of Social Theory*. London: Harvard Press.

Conklin, K. and Wellner, J. (2004) *Linking Tuition and Financial Aid Policy: The Gubernatorial Perspective*. Phoenix: WICHE.

Connidis I.A. and McMullin, J.A. (2002) Sociological ambivalence and family ties: a critical perspective, *Journal of Marriage and the Family*, 64(3): 558–67.

Connor, H. (2001) Deciding for or against participation in higher education: the views of young people from lower social backgrounds, *Higher Education Quarterly*, 55(2): 202–24.

Connor, H., Burton, R., Pearson, R., Pollard, E. and Regan, J. (1999) *Making the Right Choice: How Students Choose Universities and Colleges*. London: Universities UK.

Connor, H., Tyers, C., Modood, T. and Hillage, J. (2004) *Why the Difference? A Closer Look at Higher Education, Minority Ethnic Students and Graduates*. London: DfES.

Cooney, R. S., Rogler, L.H., Hurreell, R.M. and Ortiz, V. (1982) Decision making in intergenerational Puerto Rican families, *Journal of Marriage and the Family*, 44(3).

Cowen, R. (2000) Comparing futures or comparing pasts, *Comparative Education Review*, 36(3): 333–42.

Corrigan, P. (1992) The politics of Access courses in the 1990s, *Journal of Access Studies*, 7(1): 19–32.

Croatian Bureau of Statistics (2001) Census. Available at: http:/www.dzs.hr/ Popis%2020001/Posis/Graphs/skobarsbody.html#IDX1

Croll, P. and Moses, D. (2003) Young people's trajectories into post-compulsory

education and training: a preliminary analysis of data from the British Household Panel Survey. Paper presented at the Annual Conference of the British Educational Research Association, Heriot-Watt University, Edinburgh, 10–13 September.

Crosnoe, R. and Elder, G. H. (2002) Life course transitions, the generational stake and grandparent–grandchild relationships, *Journal of Marriage and the Family*, 644: 1089–96.

Crossley, M. (2002) Comparative and international education: contemporary challenges, reconceptualisation and new directions for the future, *ICE Online Journal* 4(2). Available at: www.tc.columbia.edu/ice

Dæhlen, M. (2000) *Innvandrere i høyere utdanning. En analyse av rekrutteringsmønsteret for ungdomskullene 1955–75 med vekt på sosial bakgrunn, kjønn og opprinnelse.* Oslo: Institutt for Sosiologi og Samfunnsgeografi, Universitetet i Oslo.

Dæhlen, M. (2001), *Usikre, dedikerte, engasjerte og distanserte. Om forventninger og motivasjon blant de nye studentene ved profesjonsstudier, Høgskolen i Oslo.* HiO-rapport 2001 nr 12.

Dasgupta, P. (2002) *Social capital and economic performance: Analytics.* Working paper. Cambridge: Faculty of Economics and Politics, University of Cambridge. Available at: www.econ.cam.ac.uk/faculty/dasgupta (accessed 15 December 2003).

Davies, R. and Elias, P. (2003) *Dropping Out: A Study of Early Leavers from Higher Education.* London: DfES.

Dearden, L., McIntosh, S., Myck, M. and Vignoles, A. (2002) The returns to academic and vocational qualifications in Britain, *Bulletin of Economic Research*, 54: 249–74.

Dearden, L., McGranahan, L. and Sianesi, B. (2004a) *The Role of Credit Constraints in Educational Choices: Evidence from NCDS and BCS70*, Discussion paper no. 48. London: Centre for the Economics of Education, London School of Economics and Political Science.

Dearden, L., McGranahan, L. and Sianesi, B. (2004b) *Returns to Education for the 'Marginal Learner': Evidence from the BCS70*, Discussion paper no. 45. London: Centre for the Economics of Education, London School of Economics and Political Science.

DEET (Department of Employment Education and Training) (1990) *A Fair Chance for All: Higher Education That's Within Everyone's Reach.* Canberra: Government Publishing Service, Australia.

Desforges, C. and Abouchaar, A. (2003) *The Impact of Parental Involvement, Parental Support and Family Education on Pupil Achievement and Adjustment: A Review of the Literature, Brief No: 433,* June. Nottingham: Department of Education and Skills.

DfEE (Department for Education and Employment) (2000) *The Excellence Challenge: The Government's Proposals for Widening the Participation of Young People in Higher Education.* London: DfEE.

DfES (2003a) *The Future of Higher Education.* London: The Stationery Office.

DfES (2003b) *Widening Participation in Higher Education.* London: The Stationery Office.

Dhillon, J. (2004) An exploration of adult learners' perspectives of using learn direct centres as sites of learning, *Research in Post-Compulsory Education*, 9(1): 147–58.

Donaldson, J. F. and Graham, S. (1999) A model of college outcomes for adults, *Adult Education Quarterly*, 50(1): 24–40.

Duru-Ballat, M. (2000) Social inequalities in the French education system: the joint effect of individual and contextual factors, *Journal of Education Policy*, 15(1): 33–40.

Ecclestone, K. Blackmore, T., Biesta, G., Colley, H. and Hughes, M. (2005) Transitions through the lifecourse: political, professional and academic perspectives. Paper presented at Annual TLRP/ESRC Conference, Warwick University.

Eckel, P. (2001) A world apart? Higher education transformation in the US and South Africa, *Higher Education Policy*, 14: 103–15.

Education and Employment Committee (2001) *Higher Education Access*, Fourth Report, HC 124. London: House of Commons.

Edwards, R. (1993) *Mature Women Students: Separating or Connecting Family and Education*. London: Taylor and Francis.

Edwards, R. (2004) Present and absent in troubling ways; families and social capital debates, *The Sociological Review*, 52(1): 1–21.

Edwards, R., Franklin, J. and Holland, J. (2003) *Families and Social Capital: Exploring the Issues*. London: Families and Social Capital ESRC Research Group, South Bank University.

Evans, K., Behrens, M., Hoffmann, B., Saxby-Smith, S. and Rudd, P. (1999) Comparative successes or failures? Some methodological issues in conducting international comparative research in post-secondary education. Paper presented at the British Educational Research Association Annual Conference, University of Sussex.

Feinstein, L. (2003) Inequality in the early cognitive development of British children in the 1970 cohort, *Economica*, 73–98.

Feinstein, L., Duckworth, K. and Sabates, R. (2004a) *A Model of the Inter-Generational Transmission of Educational Success: Wider Benefits of Learning Research*, Report 10. London: Centre for Research on the Wider Benefits of Learning, Institute of Education.

Feinstein, L., Duckworth, K. and Sabates, R. (2004b) *A Model of the Inter-Generational Effects of Parental Education: Research Brief RCB01–04*. Nottingham: Department for Education and Skills. Available at: www.dfes.gov.uk/research/ (accessed 14 October 2005).

Ferrier, F. and Heagney, M. (2001) Rethinking equity for students at Monash University, *Journal of Institutional Research*, 10(1).

Field, J. and Schuller, T. (1997) Norms, networks and trust, *Adults Learning*, 9(3): 17–18.

Forneng, S. (2003) *Swedish National Report*. Available at: www.staffs.ac.uk./access-studies

Forsyth, A. and Furlong, A. (2003) *Socio-economic Disadvantage and Access to Higher Education*. Bristol: Policy Press.

Freire, P. (1972) *Pedagogy of the Oppressed*. Harmondsworth: Penguin.

Galvin, C. (2004) 'But all the wrong people are here . . .' Wired networks, social capital and the making of public policy in a digital age. Paper presented at International Sociology of Education Conference, London, 2–4 January.

Gambetta, D. (1987) *Were they Pushed or Did They Jump? Individual Decision Mechanisms in Education*. London: Cambridge University Press.

Giddens, A. (1999) 'Family' Reith Lectures, *BBC Radio 4*, 28 April.

Gillies, V. (2003) Families and intimate relationships: a review of the sociological research, *Families and Social Capital*, ESRC Research Group Working Paper, No 2LSBU. London: ESRC.

Gorard, S. (1997) *Plugging the Gap: The Welsh School-Effect and Initial Education Trajectories, Patterns of Participation in Adult Education and Training*. Working Paper 8. Cardiff: School of Education, University of Wales, Cardiff.

Gorard, S. and Rees, G. (2002) *Creating a Learning Society?* Bristol: Policy Press.

Gorard, S., Rees, G. and Fevre, R. (1999) Patterns of participation in lifelong learning: do families make a difference? *British Educational Research Journal*, 25: 517–32.

Gorard, S., Rees, G., Fevre, R. and Welland, T. (2001) Lifelong learning trajectories: some voices of those 'in transit', *International Journal of Lifelong Education*, 20(3): 169–87.

Gorard, S., Smith, E., May, H. et al. (2006) *Review of Widening Participation Research: Addressing the Barriers to Participation in Higher Education.* Bristol: HEFCE.

Grayson, J. P. (1995) Does race matter? Outcomes of the first year experience in a Canadian university, *Canadian Journal of Higher Education*, 25(2): 78–109.

Greater Merseyside Aimhigher (2003) *Stimulating and Sustaining Interest and Achievement in Maths and Science – An Evaluative Report of the Activities of the Edge Hill Strand of Aimhigher Greater Merseyside, 2000–2002.* Greater Merseyside: Aimhigher Greater Merseyside.

Gregg, P. and Machin, S. (1997) Childhood disadvantage and success or failure in the labour market. Mimeo.

Griffin, C. (1993) *Representations of Youth: The Study of Youth and Adolescence in Britain and America.* Cambridge: Polity Press.

Griffin, C. (2000) Discourses of crisis and loss: analysing the 'Boys' Underachievement' debate, *Journal of Youth Studies*, 3(2): 167–88.

Griffin, C. (2001) Imagining new narratives of youth: youth research, the 'new Europe' and global youth culture, *Childhood*, 8(2): 147–66

Grosz, E. (1993) *Volatile Bodies: towards a Corporeal Feminism.* Bloomington: Indiana University Press.

Hammer, T. (2003) The probability for unemployed young people to re-enter education or employment: a comparative study in six northern European countries, *British Journal of Sociology of Education*, 24(2): 209–23.

Hansen, M. N. (2001) Education and economic rewards: variations by social class, origin and income measures, *European Sociological Review*, 17(3): 209–31.

Haraway, D. (1988) Situated knowledges: the science question in feminism and the privilege of partial perspective, *Feminist Studies*, 14(3): 575–99.

Hatt, S. and Baxter, A. (2003) From FE to HE: Studies in transition, *Journal of Widening Participation and Lifelong Learning*, 5(2): 18–29.

Hatt, S., Hannan, A. and Baxter, A. (2005a) Bursaries and student success: a study of students from low-income groups at two institutions in the South West, *Higher Education Quarterly*, 59(2): 111–26.

Hatt, S., Hannan, A., Baxter, A. and Harrison, N. (2005b) Opportunity Knocks? The impact of bursary schemes on students from low-income backgrounds, *Studies in Higher Education*, 30(4): 373–88.

Hramiak, A. (2001) Widening participation and ethnic minority women. Paper presented at the annual SCUTREA Conference.

Heagney, M. (2006) Widening Participation for some not others, *Journal of Widening Participation and Lifelong Learning*, 8(1): 2–3.

Heelas, P., Lash, S. and Morris, P. (1996) *Detraditionalization.* Oxford: Blackwell.

HEFCE (Higher Education Funding Council for England) (2003) *Performance Indicators in Higher Education 2000–01 and 2000–02.* Available at: www.hefce.ac.uk/learning/perfund/2003/ (accessed 3 June 2006).

HEFCE (Higher Education Funding Council for England) (2004) *Aimhigher: Guidance Notes for Integration*: Bristol: HEFCE.

HEFCE (Higher Education Funding Council for England) (2005) *Young participation in Higher Education*. Bristol: HEFCE.

Helmsley-Brown, J. (1999) College Choice: perceptions and priorities, *Educational Management and Administration*, 27(1): 85–98.

Higher Education Funding Council for England (2005) *Young Participation in Higher Education*. Bristol: Higher Education Funding Council for England.

Holdsworth, C. and Patiniotis, J. (2004) *The Choices and Experiences of Higher Education Students Living in the Family Home*. Available at: http://www.liv.ac.uk/geography/research/grants/stay_at_home.htm

Holland, J. Thompson, R. Henderson, S., McGrellis, S. and Sharpe, S. (2000) Catching on, wising up and learning from your mistakes: young people's accounts of moral development, *International Journal of Children's Rights*, 8(3): 1–24.

Horn, L. and Nunez, A-M (2000). *Mapping the Road to College: First-generation Students' Math Track, Planning Strategies, and Context for Support*. Washington, DC: NCES.

Houghton, A.M. (2005) Who needs outreach to widen participation? Families or Higher Education, in *Journal of Widening Participation and Lifelong Learning*, 7.(3).

Howieson, C. and Iannelli, C. (2003) The effects of low attainment on young people's outcomes at age 22–23 in Scotland. Paper presented at the British Educational Research Association Annual Conference, Heriot-Watt University, Edinburgh, 11–13 September.

Hramiak, A. (2001) Widening participation and ethnic minority women. Paper presented at the annual SCUTREA Conference.

James, R. (1999) *Non-traditional Students and Their University Participation: An Australian Perspective*. Canberra: DEST.

James, R. (2002) *Socioeconomic Background and Higher Education Participation: An Analysis of School Students' Aspirations and Expectations*. Canberra: DEST Higher Education Group Evaluations and Investigations Programme.

Jamieson, L. (1998) *Intimacy: Personal Relationships in Modern Societies*. Cambridge: Polity Press.

Johnston. V. (1997) *Factors influencing progression in the first year of a degree programme: results from the first year student survey*. Student retention project, internal publication, Napier University, Edinburgh.

Jones, R. (2006) 'Non-traditional' student lifecycles: Student voices and critical reflections on current widening participation policies, in D. Jary and R. Jones (eds) *Perspectives and Practice in Widening Participation in the Social Sciences*. Birmingham: Centre for Sociology, Anthropology and Politics, University of Birmingham.

Jones, R. and Thomas, L. (2005) The 2003 UK Government Higher Education White Paper: a critical assessment of its implications for the access and widening participation agenda, *Journal of Education Policy*, 20(5): 615–30.

Karen, D. (1991) The politics of class, race, and gender: access to higher education in the United States 1960–1986, *American Journal of Education*, pp. 208–37.

Kemp, D. (2000) *Higher Education Report for the 2000–2002 Triennium*. Canberra: Department of Employment, Training and Youth Affairs.

Kerkvliet, J. and Nowell, C. (2005) Does one size fit all? University differences in the influence of wages, financial aid, and integration on student retention, *Economics of Education Review*, 24(1): 85–95.

Knighton, T. (2002) Postsecondary participation:the effects of parents' education and household income, *Education Quarterly Review*, 8(3): 25–32.

Layer, G., Srivastava, A., Thomas, L. and Yorke, M. (2002) *Student Success: Building for Change*. Available at: www.actiononaccess.org/resource/aoadocs/ssintro.doc (accessed 15 June 2005).

Leathwood, C. and O'Connell, P. (2003) It's a struggle: the construction of the 'new student' in higher education, *Journal of Education Policy*, 18(6): 597–615.

Lødding, B. (2003) *Ut fra videregående. Integrasjon i arbeid og utdanning blant minoritet-sungdom i det første Reform 94-kullet* 1/2003, Oslo. (Out of upper secondary school: Integration into work and higher education among youth with minority backgrounds in the first cohort following Reform 94). Rapport 1/2003. Oslo: NIFU.

London, H. B. (1989) Breaking away: A study of first-generation college students and their families, *American Journal of Education*, 97: 144–70.

Lumby, J., Foskett, N. and Maringe, F. (2003) *Choice, Pathways and Progression for Young People in West London*. A report to London, West Learning and Skills Council, University of Lincoln.

Lynch, K. (1997), A profile of mature students in higher education and an analysis of equality issues, in R. Morris (ed.) *Mature Students in Higher Education*. Cork: Higher Education Authority Equality Unit.

Lynch, K. and O'Riordan, C. (1998) Inequality in higher education: a study of class barriers, *British Journal of Sociology of Education*, 19(4): 445–78.

Machin, S. (1998) Childhood disadvantages and intergenerational transmissions of economic status, in A.B. Atkinson and J. Hills (eds) *Exclusion, Employment and Opportunity*. CASE paper 4. London: Centre for Analysis of Social Exclusion, London School of Economics.

Mangan, J., Adnett, N. and Davies, P. (2001) Movers and stayers: determinants of post–16 educational choice, *Research in Post-Compulsory Education*, 6(1): 31–50.

Manski, C. (1989) Schooling as experimentation: a reappraisal of the post-secondary dropout phenomenon, *Economics of Education Review*, 8(4): 305–12.

McAdoo, H. P. (1978) Factors relating to stability in upwardly mobile black families, *Journal of Marriage and the Family*, 40(4): 761–76.

McCausland, W.D., Mavromaras, K. and Theodossiou, I. (2005) Explaining student retention: the case of the University of Aberdeen, *Widening Participation and Lifelong Learning*, 7(3).

McClenaghan, P. (2000) Social Capital: exploring the theoretical foundations of community development education, *British Educational Research Journal*, 26(5): 565–82.

McGrath, S. (2001) Research in a cold climate: towards a political economy of British international and comparative education, *International Journal of Educational Development*, 21: 391–400.

McGrath, S. and Millen, P. (2004) *Getting Them In: An Investigation of Factors Affecting Progression of HE of 16–19-Year-Olds in Full-Time Education*. Manchester: Manchester Metropolitan University and the LSDA.

McIntosh, S. (2003) The early post-school experiences of the unqualified/low qualified: using the labour force survey to map the 14–16 year old low achievers, Mapping the 14–16-Year-Old Demotivated Conference, London. Available at: http://cep.lse.ac.uk/events/seminars/motivation/mcintosh.pdf

McLinden, M. (2003) Children into university: an outreach project working with

school years 8–13, in D. Saunders, R. Payne, H. Jones et al. (eds) *Attracting and Retaining Learners: Policy and Practice Perspectives*. Swansea: FACE.

McNamara, O., Hustler, D., Stronach, I. et al. (2000) Room to manoevre: mobilising the 'active partner' in home school relations, *British Educational Research Journal*, 26(4): 473–491.

McPherson, M. S. and Shapiro, M. O. (1999) Reinforcing stratification in American Higher Education: some disturbing trends. Paper presented to the Malacaster Forum on Higher Education Conference, Malacaster College, June.

Metcalf, H. (2005) Paying for university: the impact of increasing costs on student employment, debt and satisfaction, *National Institute Economic Review*, 191 (January): 106–17.

Moogan, Y., Baron, S. and Harris, K. (1999) Decision-making behaviour of potential Higher Education students, *Higher Education Quarterly*, 53(3): 211–28.

Morgan, P. (1995) *Farewell to the Family: Public Policy and Family Breakdown in Britain and the USA*. London: Institute of Economic Affairs.

Morris, M., Rutt, S. and Yeshanew, T. (2005) *Pupil Outcomes One Year on. Evaluation of Aimhigher: Excellence Challenge*. Research Report RR649. London: Department for Education and Skills.

Mortenson, T. (2005) Fees – to charge or not to charge? Social engineering or social inclusion? The impact of fees and admissions policies on widening participation in HE for disadvantaged and under-represented groups. Paper presented to the European Access Network 14th Annual Conference, University of Vienna, 6–8 July.

Mortimore, P. and Whitty, G. (1999) School improvement: a remedy for social exclusion? in A. Hayton (ed.) *Tackling Disaffection and Social Exclusion: Education Perspectives and Policies*. London: Kogan Page.

Mumper, M. (1996) Beyond financial aid: alternative approaches to improving college participation, *Review of Educational Research*, 22: 83–97.

Murphy, M. (2002) Creating new demand? The development of out-reach access initiatives in higher education, *Research into Post Compulsory Education*, 7(3).

Murphy, M. and Fleming, T. (2000) Between common and college knowledge: exploring the boundaries between adult and higher education, *Studies in Continuing Education*, 22(1): 77–93.

Murray, C. (1994) *Underclass: The Crisis Deepens*. London: Institute for Economic Affairs.

NAO (National Audit Office) (2002) *Improving Student Achievement in the English Higher Education Sector*. London: The Stationery Office.

National Audit Office (2002) *Improving Student Achievement in the English Higher Education Sector*, London: Stationery Office.

Naylor, R. and Smith, J. (2002) *Schooling Effects on Subsequent University Performance: Evidence for the UK University Population*. Warwick Economic Research Papers No. 657. Coventry: Department of Economics, University of Warwick.

NCES (National Center for Education Statistics) (1988) *National Education Longitudinal Survey of 1998*. Washington, DC: NCES.

NCES (National Center for Education Statistics) (2001) Special analysis: students whose parents did not go to college: postsecondary access, persistence and attainment. Washington; DC: NCES.

Noble J. (2004) *Student Responses to Early Leaving*. Available at: www.staffs.ac.uk/institutes/access/docs/28604 uk2.doc (accessed 15 July 2006).

Novoa, A. and Yariv-Mashal, T. (2003) Comparative Research in Education: a mode

of governance or a historical journey? *Comparative Education Review* 39(4): 415–23.

NPSAS: (National Center for Educational Statistics) (2000) *National Postsecondary Student Aid Survey.* Washington DC: NPSAS.

OECD (1999) *Classifying Educational Programmes: Manual for ISCED-97 Implementation in OECD Countries 1999 Edition.* Paris: OECD.

Osborne, M. (2003) Policy and practice in widening participation: a six country comparative study of access as flexibility, *International Journal of Lifelong Education*, 22(1): 43–58.

Osborne, R. and Leith H. (2000) *Evaluation of the Targeted Initiative on Widening Access for Young People from Socio-economically. Disadvantaged Backgrounds.* Report to the Higher Education Authority. Available at: www.hea.ie.

Osborne, M. and Lumsden, M. A. (2005) Working in Health Access Programme (WHAP) – An Overview. Paper presented to the WHAP conference, University of Stirling, 1 Dec.

Osborne, M. and Thomas, E. (2003) *Lifelong Learning in a Changing Continent.* Leicester: NIACE.

Osler A. and Starkey, H. (2003) Learning for cosmopolitan citizenship: theoretical debates and young people's experiences, *Educational Review*, 55(3): 243–54.

Ozga, J. and Sukhnandan, L. (1997) *Undergraduate Non-Completion in Higher Education in England*, Report 2. Bristol: HEFCE.

Papadopoulous, G. (2000) New resourcing strategies for an inclusive higher education, in L. Thomas and M. Cooper (eds) *Changing the Culture of the Campus: Towards an Inclusive Higher Education.* Stoke-on-Trent: Staffordshire University Press.

Parker, M. and Courtney, J. (1998) Universities or nurseries? Education, professionals and taxpayers, in D. Jary and M. Parker (eds) *The New Higher Education: Issues and Directions for the Post-Dearing University.* Stoke on Trent: Staffordshire University Press.

Pennell, H., West, A. and Hind, A. (2005) Survey of higher education providers 2004, *Evaluation of Aimhigher: Excellence Challenge.* London: Department for Education and Skills.

Pitcher, J. and Purcell, K. (1998) Diverse expectations and access to opportunities: is there a graduate labour market? *Higher Education Quarterly*, 52(2): 179–203.

Plowden, B. (1967) *Children and Their Primary Schools: A Report of the Central Advisory Council for Education (England).* London: HMSO.

Postle, G., Clarke, J. and Bull, D. (1997) Equity programmes and strategies reported by the Australian Higher Education Sector, in G. Postle, J. Clarke, E. Skuja, et al. (eds) *Towards Excellence in Diversity: Educational Equity in the Australian Higher Education Sector in 1995: Status, Trends an Future Directions.* Toowomba: University of South Queensland Press.

Postle, G., Taylor, J., Taylor, J. and Clarke, J. (2000) Flexible delivery and inclusivity: pedagogical and logistical perspectives, in L. Thomas and M. Cooper, (eds) *Changing the culture of the campus: Towards and inclusive higher education.* Stoke-on-Trent: Trentham Books Ltd.

Preece, J. (1999) *Combating Social Exclusion in University Adult Education* Hampshire: Ashgate Publishing.

Preston, J. (2004) Rationing Higher Education: *A Mixed Methods Study of Economic, Cultural and Institutional Factors in Progression from Further to Higher education in*

England. Thesis submitted for the degree of Doctor of Philosophy at the University of London Institute of Education.

Prins, J. (1997) *Studie-uitval in het Wetenschappelijk Onderwijs, Studentenkenmerken en opleidingskenmerken als verklaring voor studietval.* Nijmegen: Nijmegen University Press.

Puttnam, R. D. (2000) *Bowling Alone: The Collapse and Revival of American Community.* New York: Simon Schuster.

Quinn, J. (2002) Locatable or parochial? Situating access research. Paper presented to the British Educational Research Association Conference, University of Exeter, September.

Quinn, J. (2003) *Powerful Subjects: Are Women Really Taking Over the University?* Stoke-on-Trent: Trentham Books.

Quinn, J. (2004a) Understanding working class 'drop out' from higher education through a socio-cultural lens: cultural narratives and local contexts, International Studies in Sociology of Education, 14(1): 57–75.

Quinn, J. (2004b) Mothers, learners and countermemory, *Gender and Education,* 16(3): 365–79.

Quinn, J. (2005) Belonging in a learning community: the re-imagined university and imagined social capital, *Studies in the Education of Adults,* 37(1): 4–18.

Quinn, J. (2006) Mass participation but no curriculum transformation: the hidden issue in the access to Higher Education debate, in D. Jary and R. Jones (eds) *Perspectives and Practice in Widening Participation in the Social Sciences.* Birmingham: CSAP, University of Birmingham.

Quinn et al (2006)- This is the same reference now published so you can add these details to the reference 32(5): 735–751.

Quinn, J., Thomas, L., Slack, K. et al. (2005) *From Life Crisis to Lifelong Learning: Rethinking Working Class 'Drop Out' from Higher Education.* York: Joseph Rowntree Foundation.

Quinn, J., Thomas, L., Slack, K. et al. (forthcoming) Lifting the Hood: lifelong learning and young, white, provincial working-class masculinities, *British Educational Research Journal.*

Raffe, D., Fairgrieve, K., and Martin, C. (2001) Participation, inclusiveness, academic drift and parity of esteem: a comparison of post-compulsory education and training in England, Wales, Scotland and Northern Ireland, *Oxford Review of Education,* 27 (2).

Read, B., Archer, A. and Leathwood, C. (2003) Challenging cultures? Student conceptions of 'belonging' and 'isolation' at a post-1992 university, *Studies in Higher Education,* 28(3): 261–77.

Reay, D. (1998) 'Always knowing' and 'Never being sure': Institutional and family habituses and higher education choice, *Journal of Education Policy* 13(4): 519–529.

Reay, D., David, M. and Ball, S. (2001) Making a difference? institutional habituses and higher education choice, *Sociological Research Online.* Available at: www.socresonline.org.uk/socresonline/

Reay, D., David, M.E. and Ball, S. (2005) *Degrees of Choice.* Stoke-on-Trent: Trentham Books.

Ribbens McCarthy, J., Edwards, R. and Gillies, V. (2002) *Making Families: Moral Tales of Parenting and Step Parenting.* York: Sociology Press.

Riddell, S., Wilson, A. and Tinklin, T. (2002) Disability and the wider access agenda: supporting disabled students in different institutional contexts, *Journal of Widening Participation and Lifelong Learning,* 4(3): 13–25.

Robbins, L. (1963) Higher Education Report of a Committee Cmnd 2154. London: HMSO.

Rose, N. (1996) Authority and the genealogy of subjectivity, in P. Heelas, S. Lash and P. Morris (eds) *Detraclitionalization: Critical Reflections on Authority and Identity*. Oxford: Blackwell.

Schnitzer, K. (2003) *German National Report*. Available at: www.staffs.ac.uk/access-studies.

Schuetze, H. and Slowey, M. (eds) (2000) *Higher Education and Lifelong Learning: International perspectives on change*. London: Routledge/Falmer.

Scott, P. and Smith, D. (1995) *Access and Consolidation: The Impact of Steady State on Opportunities for Non-standard Applicants to Universities and Colleges. A Second Report*. Leeds: University of Leeds Centre for Policy Studies in Education.

Simpson, O. (2003) *Student Retention in Online Open and Distance Learning*. London: Routledge/Falmer.

Simpson, O. (2006) Rescuing the personal tutor: lessons in costs and benefits, in L. Thomas, and P. Hixenbaugh (eds) *Personal Tutoring in Mass Higher Education*. Stoke-on-Trent: Trentham Books.

Skeggs, B. (2005) *Class, Self, Culture*. London: Routledge.

Skilbeck, M. and Connell, H. (2000) *Access and Equity in Higher Education: An International Perspective on Issues and Strategies*. Dublin: Higher Education Authority.

Slack, K. (2003) Whose aspirations are they anyway? *International Journal of Inclusive Education*, 7(4): 325–37.

Smart, C., Neale, B. and Wade, A. (2001) *The Changing Experience of Childhood: Families and Divorce*. Cambridge: Polity Press.

Smith, J. and Naylor, R.A. (2001) Dropping out of university: a statistical analysis of the probability of withdrawal for UK university students, *Journal of the Royal Statistical Society*, 164(2): 389–405.

Stacey, J. (1996) *In the Name of the Family: Rethinking Family Values in the Postmodern Age*. Boston: Beacon Books.

Statistics Canada (2002), *Coup d'oeil sur le Canada* (Canada at a glance), 2nd edn. Available at: www.statcan.ca/francais/freepub/12-581-XIF/12-581-XIF01001.pdf

Striplin, J. J. (2000) Facilitating transfer for first generation community college students, *ERIC digest*. Available at: www.ericdigests.org/2000

Stuart, M. (2002) *Collaborating for Change? Managing Widening Participation in Further and Higher Education*. Leicester: NIACE.

Sutton Trust (2002) A research study among 11–16 year olds on behalf of the Sutton Trust, *Schools Omnibus 2001–2002 (Wave 8)*. London: Sutton Trust.

Tan, H. and Peterson, C (1992) Postschool training of British and American youth, in D. Finegold, L. McFarland, and W. Richardson (eds) *Something Borrowed, Something Blue? A Study of the Thatcher Government's Appropriation of American Education and Training Policy*, Part 1. Wallingford: Triangle.

Tarleton, A. (2003) Wrong course, wrong time, *Guardian*, 7 March.

Taylor, R. (2000) Continuing education practice, lifelong learning and the construction of an accessible higher education in the United Kingdom, *Journal of Widening Participation and Lifelong Learning*, 2(3): 14–22.

Tett, L. (2000) 'I'm working-class and proud of it': gendered experiences of nontraditional participants in higher education, *Gender and Education*, 12(2): 183–94.

Thomas, E. (2001a) *Widening Participation in Post-compulsory Education*. London: Continuum.

Thomas, E. (2001b) Power, Assumptions and Prescriptions: A critique of widening participation policy-making, *Higher Education Policy*, 14(4): 361–76.

Thomas, L. (2002) Student retention in higher education: the role of institutional habitus, *Journal of Education Policy*, 17(4): 423–42.

Thomas, L. (2003) Building social capital to improve student success. Paper presented to the British Educational Research Association Annual Conference.

Thomas, E. and Jones, R. (2000) Policy, practice and theory: the role of higher education research in combating social exclusion, in E. Thomas and M. Cooper (eds) *Changing the Culture of the Campus: Towards an Inclusive Higher Education.* Stoke-on-Trent: Trentham Books.

Thomas, L. and Jones, R. (2003) Examining Bourdieu's concepts of capital in relation to student retention, in D. Saunders, R. Payne, H. Jones, A. Mason, and J. Storan (eds) *Attracting and Retaining Learners: Policy and Practice Perspectives.* London: FACE.

Thomas, L. and Jones, R. (2006) *Embedding Employability Throughout the Widening Participation Student Lifecycle.* York: Higher Education Academy.

Thomas, L. and Slack, K. (1999) *Evaluation of the Aim High Project.* Stoke-on-Trent: Institute for Access Studies, Staffordshire University.

Thomas, L. and Slack, K. (2000) *Evaluation of Aiming High 2000.* Stoke-on-Trent: Institute for Access Studies, Staffordshire University.

Thomas, E. and Quinn, J. (2003a) *International Insights into Widening Participation: Supporting the Success of Under-represented Groups in Tertiary Education: Final Report.* Stoke-on-Trent: Institute for Access Studies, Staffordshire University.

Thomas, L. and Quinn, J. (2003b) From a distance you can see more clearly: developing an international methodology with local benefits for student retention. Paper presented to the British Educational Research Association Conference. Edinburgh: Heriot-Watt University.

Thomas, W. and Webber, D. (2001) 'Because my friends are': the impact of peer groups on the intention to stay on at sixteen, *Research in Post-Compulsory Education*, 6(3): 339–54.

Thomas, L., Yorke, M. and Woodrow, M. (2001) *Access and Retention.* Available at: www.actiononaccess.ong/resource/aoadocs/ssrep2.doc (accessed 15 June 2005).

Thomas, L., Quinn, J., Slack, K. and Casey, L. (2002) *Student Services. Effective Approaches to Retaining Students in Higher Education.* Stafford: Institute for Access Studies, Staffordshire University.

Thomas, L., May, H., Harrop, H. et al. (2005) *From the Margins to the Mainstream: Embedding Widening Participation in Higher Education.* London: Universities UK.

Thompson, J. (2001) *Re-rooting Lifelong Learning.* Leicester: NIACE.

Thornhill, D. (2002) Widening access to higher education in Ireland, L. Thomas, M. Cooper and J. Quinn (eds) *Collaboration to Widen Participation in Higher Education.* Stoke-on-Trent: Trentham Books.

Tight, M. (1998) Education, education, education! The vision of lifelong learning in the Kennedy, Dearing and Fryer reports, *Oxford Review of Education*, 24(4): 473–85.

Tonks, D. (1999) Access to UK higher education, 1991–98: using demographics, *Journal of Widening Participation and Lifelong Learning*, 1(2): 6–16.

Tupan-Wenno, M. and Woolf, R. (2003) *Netherlands National Report.* Available at: www.staffs.ac.uk/access-studies.

UCAS (2002) *Paving the Way.* Cheltenham: UCAS.

UNICEF (2001) *The State of the World's Children.* Florence: UNICEF.

UNICEF (2002) *A League Table of Educational Disadvantage in Rich Nations,* Innocenti Report Card No. 4, November. Florence: UNICEF Innocenti Research Centre.

UNITE (2005) *Student Experience Report.* London: UNITE.

University of California (2003) *The Contribution of First-generation College Students to the University of California Learning Environment: Preliminary Results from the Spring 2003 University of California Undergraduate Experience Survey.* San Francisco: University of California. Available online.

Upshaw, W. (2003) *United States National Report.* Available at: www/staffs.ac.uk/access-studies

US Department of Education (2002) *Beginning Postsecondary Students Longitudinal Study,* 1996–2001 Data Analysis System, Washington, DC: US National Center for Education Statistics.

UUK (Universities UK) (2002) *Social Class and Participation: Good Practice in Widening Access to Higher Education.* London: UUK.

Vidacek-Hains, V. (2003) *Croatia National Report.* Available at: www.ias.staffs.ac.uk

Vidacek-Hains, V., Divjak, B. and Horvatek, R. (2004) The importance of students' active participation and communication in colleges and universities and the possible impact on achievement. Paper presented at the International Perspectives on Working Class Student Withdrawal Conference, Staffordshire University, 28 June.

Vincent, C. (2001) Social class and parental agency, *Journal of Educational Policy,* 16(4): 347–64.

Warren, D. (2002) Curriculum design in a context of widening participation in higher education, *Arts and Humanities in Higher Education,* 1(1): 85–9.

Watson, K. (1998) Memories, models and mapping: the impact of geopolitical change on comparative studies in education, *Compare,* 28(1): 5–31.

Watson, J. and Church, A. (2003) *Funding the Future: The Attitudes of Year 10 Pupils in England and Wales to Higher Education.* London: National Union of Students.

West, A., Xavier, R. and Hind, A. (2003) *Evaluation of Aimhigher: Survey of Opportunity Bursary Applications 2001/2002: Preliminary Finding,* Research Report 497. London: DfES.

Williams, J. (ed.) (1997) The discourse of access: the legitimation of selectivity, *Negotiating Access to Higher Education: The Discourse of Selectivity and Equity.* Buckingham: Open University Press/SRHE.

Wilson, F. (1997) The construction of paradox? One case of mature students in higher education, *Higher Education Quarterly,* 51(4): 347–66.

Woodrow, M. (with Lee, M., McGrane, J., Osborne, B. et al.) (1998) *From Elitism to Inclusion: Good Practice in Widening Access to Higher Education.* London: Universities UK.

Woolcock, M. (1998) Social capital and economic development: towards a theoretical synthesis and policy framework, *Theory and Society,* 27: 151–208.

Wynn-Williams, S., Chilton, H., Hallsworth, A. and Thomas, L. (1999) Overcoming impediments to educational delivery: the Staffordshire Experience, *London Journal of Canadian Studies,* 15.

Yorke, M. and Longden, B. (2004) *Retention and Student Success in Higher Education.* Maidenhead: Open University Press.

Yorke, M. and Thomas, L. (2003) Improving the retention of students from lower socio-economic groups, *Journal of Higher Education Policy and Management,* 25(1): 63–75.

Index

The Society for Research into Higher Education

The Society for Research into Higher Education (SRHE), an international body, exists to stimulate and coordinate research into all aspects of higher education. It aims to improve the quality of higher education through the encouragement of debate and publication on issues of policy, on the organization and management of higher education institutions, and on the curriculum, teaching and learning methods.

The Society is entirely independent and receives no subsidies, although individual events often receive sponsorship from business or industry. The Society is financed through corporate and individual subscriptions and has members from many parts of the world. It is an NGO of UNESCO.

Under the imprint *SRHE & Open University Press*, the Society is a specialist publisher of research, having over 80 titles in print. In addition to *SRHE News*, the Society's newsletter, the Society publishes three journals: *Studies in Higher Education* (three issues a year), *Higher Education Quarterly* and *Research into Higher Education Abstracts* (three issues a year).

The Society runs frequent conferences, consultations, seminars and other events. The annual conference in December is organized at and with a higher education institution. There are a growing number of networks which focus on particular areas of interest, including:

Access	FE/HE
Assessment	Graduate Employment
Consultants	New Technology for Learning
Curriculum Development	Postgraduate Issues
Eastern European	Quantitative Studies
Educational Development Research	Student Development

Benefits to members

Individual

- The opportunity to participate in the Society's networks
- Reduced rates for the annual conferences
- Free copies of *Research into Higher Education Abstracts*
- Reduced rates for *Studies in Higher Education*

- Reduced rates for *Higher Education Quarterly*
- Free online access to *Register of Members' Research Interests* – includes valuable reference material on research being pursued by the Society's members
- Free copy of occasional in-house publications, e.g. *The Thirtieth Anniversary Seminars Presented by the Vice-Presidents*
- Free copies of *SRHE News* and *International News* which inform members of the Society's activities and provides a calendar of events, with additional material provided in regular mailings
- A 35 per cent discount on all SRHE/Open University Press books
- The opportunity for you to apply for the annual research grants
- Inclusion of your research in the *Register of Members' Research Interests*

Corporate

- Reduced rates for the annual conference
- The opportunity for members of the Institution to attend SRHE's network events at reduced rates
- Free copies of *Research into Higher Education Abstracts*
- Free copies of *Studies in Higher Education*
- Free online access to *Register of Members' Research Interests* – includes valuable reference material on research being pursued by the Society's members
- Free copy of occasional in-house publications
- Free copies of *SRHE News* and *International News*
- A 35 per cent discount on all SRHE/Open University Press books
- The opportunity for members of the Institution to submit applications for the Society's research grants
- The opportunity to work with the Society and co-host conferences
- The opportunity to include in the *Register of Members' Research Interests* your Institution's research into aspects of higher education

Membership details: SRHE, 76 Portland Place, London W1B 1NT, UK Tel: 020 7637 2766. Fax: 020 7637 2781. email: srheoffice@srhe.ac.uk world wide web: http://www.srhe.ac.uk./srhe/ *Catalogue:* SRHE & Open University Press, McGraw-Hill Education, McGraw-Hill House, Shoppenhangers Road, Maidenhead, Berkshire SL6 2QL. Tel: 01628 502500. Fax: 01628 770224. email: enquiries@openup.co.uk – web: www.openup.co.uk

RETENTION AND STUDENT SUCCESS IN HIGHER EDUCATION
Mantz Yorke and Bernard Longden

- What is the policy background to current interest in retention and student success?
- What causes students to leave institutions without completing their programmes?
- How can theory and research help institutions to encourage student success?

Retention and completion rates are important measures of the performance of institutions and higher education systems. Understanding the causes of student non-completion is vital for an institution seeking to increase the chances of student success.

The early chapters of this book discuss retention and student success from a public policy perspective. The later chapters concentrate on theory and research evidence, and on how these can inform institutional practices designed to enhance retention and success (particularly where students are enrolled from disadvantaged backgrounds).

This book draws upon international experience, particularly from the United Kingdom, Australia, South Africa and the United States.

Retention and Student Success in Higher Education is essential reading for lecturers, support staff, and senior managers in higher education institutions, and for those with a wider policy interest in these matters.

Contents
Prologue – Setting the scene – Student retention: A macro perspective from South Africa – Access and retention in Australian higher education – Access and retention in English higher education: A parliamentary perspective – Institutional performance – Theory: A multiplicity of perspectives – Reconceptualizing antecedents of social integration in student departure – Why students leave their programmes – Succeeding against the demographic odds – Promoting student success – Epilogue – References – Indices.

200pp   0 335 21274 3 (Paperback)   0 335 21275 1 (Hardback)